THOMAS NELSON AND SONS LTD
Parkside Works Edinburgh 9
36 Park Street London W1
312 Flinders Street Melbourne C1

302–304 Barclays Bank Building
Commissioner and Kruis Streets
Johannesburg

THOMAS NELSON AND SONS (CANADA) LTD
91–93 Wellington Street West   Toronto 1

THOMAS NELSON AND SONS
19 East 47th Street New York 17

SOCIÉTÉ FRANÇAISE D'EDITIONS NELSON
97 rue Monge Paris 5

———

Printed in Great Britain by Thomas Nelson and Sons Ltd, Edinburgh

GREEKS

BY MICHAEL GRANT
AND DON POTTINGER

THOMAS NELSON & SONS LTD.

FOREWORD

While the other inhabitants of Europe were still squelching savagely in their marshes or otherwise failing to conquer their environment, the Greeks, in many parts of the Mediterranean world, were creating an immeasurably more brilliant way of life, in many ways the most brilliant that the world has ever seen. It is largely due to them that the other peoples of the west gradually raised themselves out of their squalor towards lives that were more worth living.

Greek civilisation surged forward in this unprecedented fashion under the impact of older civilisations in the Near and Middle East ; and we have included in this book reminders of the new knowledge that modern research has provided about those early days. We have also tried to show in a short space how the Greeks stamped and transformed these borrowings with their own individuality, and how the product of this fusion was the famous glory of classical Greece : how it came about, how it was good and how it was bad, and what happened to it. And much of this story is remarkably relevant to our problems today.

Spanning two thousand years of every sort of vigorous effort—intellectual, moral, emotional, physical, imperial and commercial—the ancient Greeks by the miraculous rationality which they often attained were able to crystallise their wide experience of success and failure into general principles. They possessed an altogether new understanding of what the human mind could achieve, and a uniquely articulate capacity to transmit their rapidly growing experience from one generation to another. Of our own total heritage this experience forms an indispensable part ; and the artistic achievements that went with it are still among the most exciting that there have ever been.

Many Greek personalities are the earliest in the world to appear distinctly before us. They stand out of the past in the compelling clarity of their thoughts and actions : enemies of dullness, nobly original, living life to the full. Nor were they without humour, so our illustrations, adapting certain of the methods of their vase-paintings, are less solemn than is customary.

Of that partly similar and partly different people, the Greeks of today, we have said nothing ; for to have treated them as an appendage to their predecessors, who are the subject of this book, would have done them an injustice.

We should like to thank Professors David Talbot Rice and Stuart Piggott and Mr Michael Gough for their helpful advice.

MICHAEL GRANT AND DON POTTINGER

CONTENTS

PART ONE
4000 - 1000 B.C.

THE GREEKS ARRIVE

Primitive Greeks come from the north to the land we now call Greece—they learn of Crete's advanced maritime civilisation—they borrow from it to establish imperial Mycenae—Crete succumbs to Mycenae—Mycenae is over-run by a final wave of Greek invaders, the Dorians.

BEFORE THE GREEKS

More than five thousand years ago, the land which we now call Greece was inhabited by people who ground and polished their stone tools and made painted pottery. They scraped a living in villages near arable land where there was a river or a spring ; and these are not very frequent in Greece, where four-fifths of the country is barren today. Without the leisure necessary for civilisation to develop, they passed thousands of years entirely engrossed in the daily struggle for food.

About 3000 B.C. their dwellings were destroyed by invaders whose bronze tools enabled men to work more quickly, and life became slightly less hard. The invaders may have come from Asia Minor. They spoke a language, probably not Indo-European, which survived in words ending in -ssos, -nthos.

THRACE

GREECE

AEGEAN SEA

DARDANELLES
•TROY

NAUPACTUS PARNASSUS
DELPHI

BOEOTIA

ATTICA

ASIA
MINOR

CORINTHOS•
MYCENAE•
TIRYNS•

PELOPONNESE

PYLOS

•HALIKARNASSOS

CNOSSOS•
CRETE

*thalassa
= sea*

In the naturally more fertile regions of the Near and Middle East—Egypt, Sumeria on the Persian Gulf, Mesopotamia and Crete—life was easier and civilisation a great deal farther advanced.

CRETE

In Crete the soil and climate were better than on the mainland, and produced ship timber and a surplus of wine and oil. The scattered communities of the island, non-Greeks whose ancestors may have come from Asia Minor, had been established from the fourth millennium. In about 2000 B.C. they coalesced into a single kingdom with its capital at Cnossus. This city of some 100,000 inhabitants was connected by paved roads to the rest of the island and was the centre of Cretan sea-borne trade to every part of the eastern Mediterranean.

Cretan harbour towns foreshadow modern urban communities

Cretan civilisation is called "Minoan" after its legendary sea king Minos

Minos is the earliest ruler known to us who possessed a "fleet" (Thucydides)

Secure in their sea-power, the priest kings of Cnossus had no need to fortify their luxurious stone palace. This palace, so complex that it became the "labyrinth" of legend, extended over five acres of cloistered courts, pillared halls, stairways and terraces on many levels, and stored the kingdom's wealth in many great storehouses with elaborate inventories.

Cnossus had very advanced water sanitation and drains

The architecture of this building recalls the far earlier palaces of Sumeria

The Cretans chiefly worshipped goddesses, including forerunners of Athena, Hera and Artemis ; though they also seem to have worshipped Zeus as a year-god—male child of Mother Earth.

Earliest known appearance of divinities later found in Greece

Women were probably held in high esteem in ancient Crete

With the prosperity resulting from their sea trade, the Cretans had leisure to develop a brilliant, imaginative and lively civilisation. Their best wheel-turned pottery and their fresco paintings show a vivid, sophisticated blend of abstraction, naturalism, and confident impressionism quite different from the austere, deliberate art of Egypt from which they had learned. Their crowd scenes, notably of women at what is probably the first theatre—where they watched religious processions, athletics, music and dancing—are masterpieces of human observation.

Cretan dress and hairstyle was Egyptian, and Cretans appear in Egyptian sculptures

Ceramic decoration is Crete's most obvious legacy to later Greece

Octopus pot

They also liked to paint animals and birds in natural settings ; their art shows profound sympathy with nature and its movement. Their bull ceremonies were breathtaking in their daring and highly trained skill.

These are paintings in the modern sense, relating background to figures

Girls as well as young men were bull-vaulters

9

THE GREEKS ARRIVE

The early Greeks were organised in strong patriarchal families

Homer's heroes eat an ox every 2,000 verses, but the usual Attic dinner had two courses— porridge and porridge

The first wave of Greeks reached Greece during the migrations of peoples about 2000 B.C., when the foundations of Europe and the Near East were established on the basis of peasant agriculture and simple metal-working techniques. Speaking a language something like Greek, these invaders or immigrants settled in almost all parts of Greece, causing violent changes and subjugating or overshadowing the inhabitants.

It is hard to distinguish them in race from the peoples to the east of them; a distinction between "Greeks" and "Asiatics" is too simple

They may have come originally from the steppe-lands of South Russia. Their material culture closely resembles that of contemporary Troy, which according to one recent theory may have been just as Greek as they were themselves.

Human remains at Troy show much race mixture (and high mortality)

Homer's Greeks and Trojans have much the same language, gods and conventions

They introduced houses originally designed for more wintry climates; oblong, porched, fenced dwellings with a hearth in the centre of the floor and a gabled roof with a hole to let out the smoke. This sort of house (megaron) seems to imitate a timber form originating from the forests of northern and eastern Europe.

The megaron, though coming from a region of snow and ice, was the origin of the later Greek temples. It also appears very early in Anatolia.

The hearth is "Vesta" in Latin, "Hestia" in Greek. Fire is "Ignis" in Latin, "Agni" in Sanskrit

The Greeks also brought with them the use of the potter's wheel, and made a new sort of scaly-surfaced pottery with shapes imitated from metal-work. This has been found, for example, at Orchomenus in the small lush plain of Boeotia— "land of cows" (few parts of Greece were fertile enough to support cattle).

Called "Minyan" ware, after Minyas, legendary founder of Orchomenus

Later Greek hero cults and mythology probably originate with these early immigrants

These Greeks worshipped Zeus, Lord of the Sky, and practised a cult of the dead. Later, idols and animal figurines were abundant in their tombs—especially in the poorer ones where they were substitutes for real gifts.

With better tools than their predecessors, and better soil, forests and game than today, they won for themselves a certain amount of leisure and rapidly progressed to new military strength.

MYCENAEAN CIVILISATION

Mycenae anticipates the typical siting of later Greek cities

This partly novel, partly derivative culture reached its material climax in the great royal fortresses in the Peloponnesian peninsula of south Greece. Their civilisation takes its name from the city of Mycenae. It lay on a spur, near a fertile strip, far enough from the Aegean Sea to escape surprise by pirates. Its central fortress on the summit of the hill commanded roads leading south to the Aegean Sea and north to the Isthmus of Corinth.

Control was in the hands of those who owned the soil. But they were no longer farmers, and they monopolised powerful new armaments—long bronze rapiers, huge shields and light horse-drawn chariots of oriental origin.

"Mycenae, a fortress rich in gold and other wealth" (Homer)

Schliemann also discovered the site of Troy

They were able to acquire wealth from faraway lands, such as ivory from Syria derived from elephant hunts farther east. The enormous wealth of Mycenae in about 1600 B.C. was revealed when the German archaeologist Schliemann in 1876 discovered the royal graves within the citadel. The graves, which had not—like so many—been robbed in ancient times, yielded a fabulous quantity of gold and other precious objects. Corpses of royal children were wrapped completely in sheet gold.

Like Scythian art of 1,000 years later

Their art reflects the origins of these Greek invaders in the steppes. There are many vivid animal scenes which recall the widespread "animal style" of the early Eurasian steppes, the "Art of the Northern Nomads". There are close anticipations of Mycenae in the spectacular tombs of another invading royal house across the Aegean. This was at Alacahüyük, capital of the powerful non-Indo-European Hattian state which dominated the Anatolian plateau before

Silver and gold bull's head, with sun symbol, from royal grave at Mycenae

The Hittite rulers probably arrived in Anatolia during the same series of movements which brought the Greeks to Greece

Both Mycenaeans and Hittites show features in common with the cultures of primitive Germany

the Indo-European Hittite régime overthrew it. At Alacahüyük, as at Mycenae, the tombs are roofed by beams set on low walls, and offerings were probably made on their roofs. The battle-axes in these Middle Bronze Age tombs provide a link with our own Wessex Bronze Age (c. 1800 B.C.).

Hittite stag

Mycenaean stag

Scythian stag

⟨ 2000–1500 B.C. ⟩

The earliest cremation burials yet recognised in the Aegean area (1750-1600 B.C.) have recently been discovered at Cnossus ; Greeks seem to have reached the island early

Earlier Cretan inscriptions are in "Linear A", probably a non-Greek language

For several centuries the early Greeks of the mainland of what is now Greece were increasingly influenced by the superior trading civilisation of Crete, not far from their south-east coast. As they grew in power the princes of Mycenae and other fortresses bought more and more splendid weapons, ornaments and precious vases from Crete and employed Cretan artists to work for them in Greece.

Greek valleys and harbours mostly happen to face south towards Crete

But by 1500 B.C. they were influencing Cretan civilisation in their turn, and even somehow extended their rule and language over the whole island for about fifty years. Thousands of clay writing tablets found at Cnossus and at the mainland Greek centres of Mycenae, Pylos, Tiryns and other towns are written in a script called "Linear B". This has recently been interpreted as an early form of the Greek language, "Old Achaean".

Mycenaean-looking tombs, goblets, etc.

The Greek government at Cnossus fell in about 1400 B.C., and the great palace was destroyed, probably by a rebellion of the Cretans against their Greek overlords—whose great Cretan fleet would have been strong enough to stop any invader.

Command of the seas then passed from Crete to mainland monarchs —linked to one another by ties of varying strength—of whom the kings of Mycenae were among the most powerful. In the next two centuries Mycenaean Greeks spread all over the Mediterranean, establishing settlements, fortified colonies and trading connections. Mycenae was now a great power among the other Near Eastern great powers. The Greeks had become a major seafaring nation.

They also traded with the independent city of Troy, on the Dardanelles

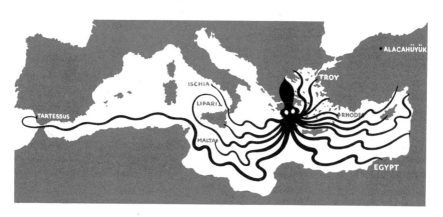

ZENITH OF MYCENAE

The art of Mycenae had developed greatly under strong Cretan influence. But its huge-scale buildings and monumental sculpture are alien to Crete. The massive Lion Gate of Mycenae's citadel recalls the architecture of Asia Minor and Syria, not Crete. Mycenaean vases of buff pottery with lustrous brown ornament are based on Cretan models but foreshadow the Greek feeling for structural values and proportion ; they show few signs of the Cretan love for fluid movement. These vases were distributed far afield by Mycenaean trade, and dominated the Mediterranean market in the fourteenth century B.C.

Unlike the Cretans, the Mycenaeans loved hunting and chariot-racing. Their culture was magnificent, but less lively and sophisticated than Crete's ; the Cretans would not have allowed food-remnants to pile up on their floors. But writing may have been fairly widespread on the mainland by the early thirteenth century B.C. During this period Mycenae itself became an immensely strong fortified royal residence, with wells and cisterns and with quarters for the court, officials, guards and servants. The civilian population, including many rich householders, lived round the fortress in open townships ; but in times of crisis there was room for them all within the solid walls, ten to twenty-five feet thick. The neighbouring fortress of Tiryns had equally massive walls and was approached by ramp so that attackers were forced to expose their unshielded right sides. These fortresses, and Nestor's Pylos where many foreign slaves were recorded on clay tablets, became centres of small but powerful land empires—controlled by the kings' formidable war-chariots operating over roads specially built for them.

*Like mediaeval
European castle
and village*

*The ancient full-
length shield had
been replaced by
a small round
shield worn on
the left arm*

*Pylos records at
least 645 women
slaves, 370 girls,
210 boys ;
1 skilled woman
slave was worth
10 oxen*

⟨ 1800–1200 B.C. ⟩

MYCENAE CONQUERS TROY

Homer also reflects the brilliance of the Minoans and some of their material culture, but not their inner life

In the late fourteenth century B.C. the art of Mycenae became more stylised and conventional, its goods became cheap and nasty, and its wealth began to decline. The export of Mycenaean Greek wares to Egypt and the Levant ceased abruptly about 1250–20 B.C. Some have thought this was due to grave internal disturbances on the Greek mainland at this time, retained in tradition as the stories of the *Seven Against Thebes* and of Atreus and Thyestes. The material background of Homer's *Iliad* partly reflects these last years of Mycenaean power.

But this was a time of mighty upheavals, migrations, and many confused invasions among the Aegean and Near Eastern peoples. Though historical evidence is fragmentary, five "Sea Peoples" joined the King of Libya in a formidable attack on Egypt (*c.* 1220 B.C.). They included the "Ekwesh" (KWSH); there are fairly substantial reasons for believing that these invading warriors were the "Achaeans"—Homer's name for the Greeks. Whether they came from the mainland or the isles or Asia Minor is not known. The "Ahhiyawa" described as enemies on Hittite inscriptions of Asia Minor were probably Achaeans also.

We know of their attack from the Karnak inscription. The Sea Peoples also include the Etruscans, next found in western Italy

Egyptians recorded the "Drdny", probably Trojans (Dardanians), as their enemies and the allies of the Hittites at the Battle of Kadesh, about 1286 B.C.

In about 1200 B.C. a further mass of Greek invaders besieged and burnt Troy itself, where there had been six earlier successive settlements. This historical event, confirmed by archaeologists, inspired the heroic stories of the *Iliad*. Homer himself, however, did not live and compose his works for another four hundred years, during which—while knowledge of writing fluctuated and singers may often not have been literate—the epic was orally transmitted from bard to bard, like the Norse and German sagas.

The Homeric king, a great man chosen for practical co-ordination and discipline, derived from early Asia (e.g. Sumeria)

So the *Iliad* hands down not only the distant events of the siege of Troy but also many accretions from the intervening centuries (and Homer even reflects the world of his own contemporary noble patrons). Yet there is some truth in the picture he gives of the Mycenaean Greek besiegers as a loose confederacy of proud, recalcitrant, meat-fed chiefs, jealous of their reputations, under their overlord Agamemnon. Possibly they already believed in the Olympian gods as a similar loose confederacy under Zeus.

The Hittite law-code likewise reflects the idea of the king as primus inter pares with his nobles. But his position rested on divine sanction

⟨ 1350–1200 B.C. ⟩

DORIAN INVADERS

The Phrygians, with their empire in the west central region of Asia Minor, were descended from these invaders

In about the same generation as the Trojan War, there was another series of migrations. Tribes speaking Indo-European languages passed through Thrace and crossed over to Asia Minor. They brought down the Hittite empire in Asia Minor, and with it the elaborate nexus of Mycenaean relationships with the states of that peninsula. The last Hittite historical inscriptions (*c.* 1260–1200 B.C.) before this disaster already tell of wars and pirates on the Aegean coasts, and of interference from the newcomers in the most westerly Hittite dependencies.

Possibly these great mass migrations in the Balkans started in Hungary

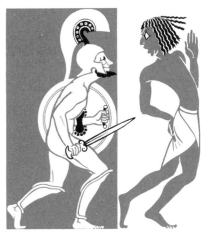

Later Greeks explained the Danaoi as a dynasty of oriental origin established at Argos. They may have come there from southern Asia Minor or Cyprus

Then, early in the twelfth century B.C., Syria and Egypt were invaded with terrible destruction by two unprecedentedly large hordes of migrant Sea Peoples (*c.* 1175 B.C.). They swept down from Asia Minor, with their goods and families following in ox-carts. The first attack shows some co-ordinating policy, for it was made by land and by sea ; the second attack was mainly naval. These Sea Peoples are listed in the Egyptian inscriptions at Medinet Habu, and include the Philistines and the "Danuna". After much scholarly discussion it seems permissible to identify these "Danuna" with the "Danaoi"—which is another Homeric name for the Greeks.

Within a century of these aggressive expeditions, the palace of the Mycenaeans was destroyed. It fell to other Greeks—backward relations, the last stream of Greek invaders—probably of much the same racial mixture and Indo-European tongue as themselves. These "Dorians" (*c.* 1150–1100 B.C.), perhaps pressed by even more barbarous hordes of Illyrians behind them, passed through the Balkans into northern Greece, pushing before them earlier Greek arrivals (Aeolians and Ionians) who migrated to the coasts of Asia Minor.

The Ionians had been in north-western Greece ; they moved east via Attica

Later Greek legend told that King Codrus of Athens sacrificed himself by quarrelling with Dorians to fulfil a prophecy and save his city

After a time the Dorians crossed the Gulf of Corinth into the Peloponnese in two main streams : an eastern stream in the middle part of the Gulf and another at its western extremity. The invaders occupied or subdued almost all of the Peloponnese except mountainous Arcadia in the centre. The eastern stream, after passing via Delphi, where the priesthood became, and remained, a Dorian prerogative, crossed the Gulf at Naupactus (meaning "ship construction"). Other Dorians finally reached Crete, Rhodes and south-western Asia Minor.

⟨ 1250–1000 B.C. ⟩

The Dorian invaders came wearing the loose cloak, *himation*, that was to become the typical feature of Greek dress, and the "spectacle" fibula. With them, too, or in their wake shortly afterwards, came more significant changes in Greek life. Cremation definitely replaced burial of the dead. And in the eleventh century B.C. or at the end of the twelfth, the use of iron began in Greece : the iron slashing sword began to play a formidable part.

*The Dorians
had little
mythology of
their own,
and adopted
Heracles, the
most popular
of all Greek
heroes, as
their ancestor*

*Homer refers to
cremation and
iron axes,
knives and
arrow-heads, but
not explicitly
to iron swords*

Iron may first have been employed in Greece owing to the failure of bronze supplies when the Greeks lost control of the seas, after the fall of Mycenae, to the Phoenician navies of Sidon and later of Tyre. Mass production had revolutionary possibilities. The first large state to recognise them had probably been Mitanni in the Khabur valley of Syria. Mitanni, momentarily powerful in the fifteenth century B.C., had adapted to military purposes the process for the bulk production of iron invented in the Armenian highlands to its north—although iron was already widely known in small quantities at a much earlier period.

*The site of the
Mitanni capital,
Wash'shukkani,
has not been
found*

*Sidon and Tyre
survived
the migrations*

This made wars even more terrible and tools much more readily available, as iron ore was more abundant and the metal more easily extracted than the components of bronze. Also, being harder than bronze, iron tools lasted much longer and were more efficient. When the process crossed from Asia Minor to reach Greece some centuries after its discovery, these tools gave the masses and especially the rural workers a real share in the advantages of civilisation.

A farmer could now much more easily break ground, clear it of trees and scrub, dig channels for drainage and irrigation, till the soil and increase his production. As he relied more on his own efforts he became less dependent on the state, the monarch and the priesthood.

PART TWO
1000 - 500 B.C.
THE GREEK
CHARACTER EMERGES

The early centuries are hard to reconstruct—politically the
Greeks remain divided—except in Sparta, the tiny republican
city-state emerges as the normal unit, and its law, religion and
newly invented coinage spread widely—poetry and art pro-
liferate—there is rapid progress toward a scientific viewpoint.

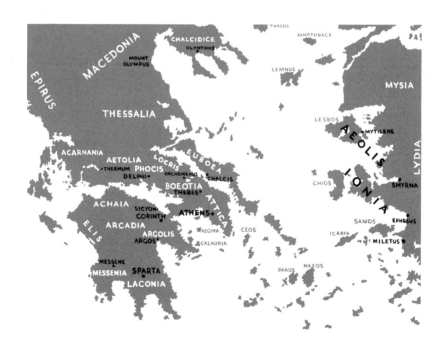

A DARK AGE?

Overseas trade
almost ceased

"Go to sea if you
must, but only
from June to
September . . .
and even then
you will be a
fool" (Hesiod)

The destruction of the palaces of Mycenae, Tiryns and Pylos plunged Greece into its "Dark Age". At least our knowledge of the period is dark, since for the first three centuries of the last millennium B.C. we have little historical, archaeological or linguistic evidence. There is no external commentary either, since the Greeks of the early Iron Age, having lost control of the sea, were cut off from the rest of the world. There were evidently sharp changes of political régime, but opinions still differ as to the extent and profundity of the break between the pre-Dorian Late Bronze Age and the Dorian Early Iron Age. It was thought that the break was very severe, but there are now reasons for supposing that there was a fair measure of continuity.

Corinth and Orchomenus, formerly Mycenaean centres, were of some importance very soon after the Dorian invasion ; and recent excavations at Mycenae itself have revealed graves which actually bridge the transition between the two (artificially constituted) epochs. So Mycenae and the other cities, though now less powerful, were still inhabited ; probably habitation had never ceased. In some other parts of Greece, such as Attica, there were no serious shocks. So it is possible that the Dark Age was not a period of complete collapse.

Bellerophon
unwittingly
carried to the
King of Lydia
a letter
requesting his
own death
(Homer, Iliad)

Shrines at
Karphi in
Crete and
Thermum in
Aetolia seem
to go back to
the tenth
century B.C.

However, in a country now containing many fairly savage Dorians, writing probably became less used—although as no inhabited site of the period has been excavated, and not a single intact substructure of a royal palace reported, it would be premature to suppose that "Linear B" script went out of use completely. If people do not build durable houses or bury their dead in luxuriously furnished tombs, the spade cannnot uncover colourful details about their lives. Yet there are traces from this epoch of houses of the old Mycenaean type. And there are temples also.

Across the Aegean, too, in Ionia, though its chief city Miletus had been engulfed after the fall of Mycenae by invaders from the hinterland, an oval house recently discovered at Smyrna is not later than about 900 B.C., and less than a century later an Ionian school of pottery was active.

POTTERS AND POETS

Transitional pottery is known as sub-Mycenaean (? c. 1100) and Proto-Geometric (? c. 1085-875 B.C.)

The first Iron Age pottery found at Smyrna has strong affinities with the vases of Attica, which were now pre-eminent. Athenian "Geometric" pottery was made from about 1000-700 B.C. It develops directly from the schematic designs of the transition from Mycenaean days, but there are new and richer patterns—for example the Maeander-pattern now covers the whole of a vase in horizontal bands. There are also scenes in silhouette—chariot and funeral processions. The vases were religious in purpose and are found in the graves of the dead.

Attic Geometric amphora

Some of the figures on the vases appear to represent statues. We have the stone base of a very early life-size statue from Samos, and a figure of Apollo from Amyclae (near Sparta) seems to go back to the eighth century. So does the temple of Artemis Orthia outside Sparta; and Hera's great temple at Argos (which had superseded its neighbour Mycenae) is of about the same period.

Apollo of Amyclae is represented on Roman coins

St Paul had trouble with the Artemisium (temple of Diana of the Ephesians)

Across the water, the same deities had shrines of equal antiquity: the Artemisium at Ephesus and the Heraeum at Samos. We have dim traditions of early religious-commercial leagues centred around such shrines. For example, a maritime league of seven city-states was called the Calaurian League after Poseidon's temple at Calauria off the east coast of the Peloponnese; Eretria (Euboea) and Orchomenus were prominent members. It also seems probable that there was an early league of Ionian cities. Homer is likely to have been an Ionian of about the eighth century B.C.; perhaps he recited the *Iliad* and the *Odyssey* at one of the great religious festivals which had now begun.

The Homeric poems show resemblances to the orally transmitted Gilgamesh epic (third millennium B.C.)

Hesiod has been compared as prophet of justice with the later Israelite Amos. But whereas to the Jews other peoples' gods were false, the early Greeks identified them with their own gods

Another early poet (his date is unknown) is Hesiod, author of "Works and Days" and the "Theogony". His parents migrated from Asia Minor to Boeotia on the mainland. His account of the universe inaugurates cosmological theory, and he originates the Greek vein of ethical speculation. He contributed to Greek humanism by stressing divine concern with human justice, an idea rarely found in Homer. Hesiod reflects a grim, hard-working, impoverished agricultural life; his standardised techniques of vine and olive growing and his rustic calendar embody the lore of many preceding centuries.

Oil, wine and corn are the basic products of Greece

REPUBLICAN GOVERNMENTS

Greek rivers are alternately trickles and roaring torrents

I solated in Greece by their loss of sea power, the Greeks were also generally isolated from each other by their broken mountainous terrain. The considerable measure of control which the Mycenaean and similar monarchies had enforced could no longer be exercised effectively. So local independence was widely asserted.

At Athens in later times the family of the Medontidae (to which Solon and Plato belonged) was traditionally regarded as the former royal house

Except at a few centres such as Sparta, where monarchy survived, local kings were first weakened and then superseded by their aristocratic councils, which formed governments by the hereditary few, the landowners who headed the clans. At Athens, for example, kingship gave place to the rule of three *archons*, aristocrats elected by the aristocracy, one of whom was the head of the former royal house ; they held hereditary office for life. During the eighth century B.C. the three archons were appointed every ten years, and after 683 B.C. annually. By now all rights of the royal family had disappeared except certain formal religious functions.

Kingship survived in the Graeco-oriental states of Cyprus

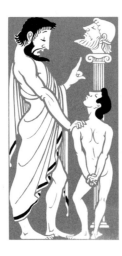

"It is in the hands of high-born men that there resteth the good piloting of cities, while they pass from father to son" (Pindar, early fifth century B.C.)

Religion had been conducted and controlled by the kings, and with their decline there remained no widespread professional priesthood. The State religion was in the hands of laymen—poets and thinkers—who prepared the way for the rise of free thought and philosophy. Once the divine authority of the kingship was destroyed, the chief remaining source of authority was the patriarchal headship of a clan—and the wealth from landowning that accompanied it. This aristocratic tradition of the early Greek states (later rationalised as the rule of "the best men" in character, not only by birth) continued to be a persistent element in Greek life and thought.

Domestic ancestor-cult linked the living members of the clan with their dead

THE CITY-STATES

The "polis" is the totality of all the citizens

"Men are the polis"

Some towns had survived the Dorian invasion, and in about the eighth century B.C. the city-state (*polis*) emerges, or re-emerges, as the normal unit of Greek society as it had been thousands of years before in Mesopotamia. In Greece development was quickest in the areas where there was most to learn from the past, for example near Mycenae, in Boeotia, and in Crete.

"Man is a political animal" (Aristotle) i.e. exists through the "polis"

Towns often formed for protection around a citadel (*acropolis*), usually a safe distance inland. Sometimes the city-states developed from single villages—elsewhere, as at Athens and Sparta, the new state controlled and absorbed the government of several villages. Each community possessed a strip of arable watered land; each had its own religious centre (the State hearth in the Council chamber) and—unlike eastern towns—its own central space (*agora*) for markets and meetings, its own theatre and gymnasium.

The total area of each state was usually very small. Athens had 1,000 square miles, Corinth 350, Chios 300, and Boeotian cities (except Thebes) averaged 70. Ceos, an island of 39 square miles, comprised four city-states entirely independent of one another. The Dorian invaders of Crete divided into forty city-states. Cyprus had seven (later ten).

Separatism was favoured by the inefficiency of siege-craft. The idea of Greek nationality only grew slowly

In historic times the only Greek communities with a population of more than 20,000 full citizens were Athens and two Sicilian cities, Syracuse and Acragas. Plato thought the ideal number was 5,000, and Aristotle said every citizen ought to know every other by sight. In addition to citizens, slaves and resident aliens (*metoikoi, perioikoi*), there were two free non-citizen classes, often outnumbering the citizens, (1) the "community-servers" (*demiourgoi*), artisans and professionals—smiths, potters, carpenters, minstrels, physicians and seers; and (2) the serfs (*thetes, penestai, helots*), hired labourers and dependants.

Land communications between cities were often bad, and political relations worse. Each clung to its own dialects and specialities. Almost all of them wasted an immense amount of energy in quarrelling and fighting with neighbouring cities. All the city-states were always governed by immediate self-interest; and the interests of the country were subordinated to those of the town.

〈1000–650 B.C.〉

ART FROM THE EAST

There are several distinct schools of Proto-Corinthian pottery

Late in the eighth century B.C. the isolation of Greece began to end : Phoenicia's monopoly of the seas was challenged. New orientalising motifs flooded into Greek art. In vase paintings new floral patterns—animals and winged monsters—replace geometric designs, and there are experiments in technique : outline drawing, polychromy, incision of lines, greater naturalism of the human form (silhouette is partly replaced by line treatment), and the inclusion of battles and mythological scenes. The method is representational and illustrative. This was long familiar in Egypt and Assyria, but in Greece these tendencies released new creative forces, formed a new Greek personality, and introduced wider variety. There were now several flourishing schools, the most famous and long-lived being at Corinth.

By 600 B.C. super-life-size statues were made in Attica under aristocratic patronage

The air of extreme simplicity is deceptive ; Greek art is always a form of wisdom ("sophia") with rules to be learnt. The "simple" modelling of surfaces is subtle and calculated, giving an impression of tautness and vitality

Our earliest surviving Greek statues are of the seventh century B.C. ; by the end of the century large-scale sculpture had begun. The Dorians of the Peloponnese and Crete took the lead. Their models were Egyptian : they used the conventionally posed Egyptian man and retained the attitude without change for a century (gods and goddesses being only distinguishable by their attributes) : but during that period, though naturalism is always controlled by stylised formalism, sculptors displayed an increasingly keen curiosity about the structure of the human body.

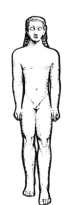

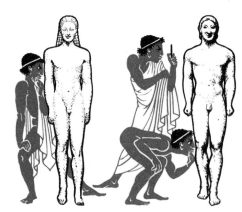

ARCHITECTURE: ALPHABET

POST AND
BEAM

In the eighth and seventh centuries B.C. the Greek temple as we know it took shape: for buildings were now more often of stone, instead of wood. Its construction, characteristic of Greek architecture, was strictly governed by "post and beam" and by stress on horizontals. The earliest surviving temples of the seventh century are Dorian: the Doric columns and triglyph frieze are a traditional form with their origins in wood, displaying Minoan and Mycenaean influences. The full development of the graceful Ionic order, the true style of Greek Asia, took place in the first half of the sixth century, about fifty years after the Doric: the Ionic capital is of obscure origin, but it seems to echo themes in Hittite and Iranian reliefs.

Triglyph: block with three vertical grooves

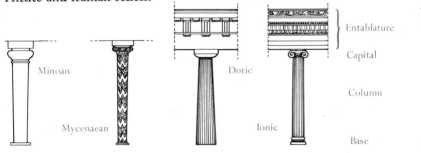

Minoan

Mycenaean

Doric

Ionic

Entablature

Capital

Column

Base

The "Order" of the facade

The Hittites had used 100 cuneiform (wedge shaped) signs and 80 hieroglyph signs (figures of objects standing for words, syllables or sounds)

Literacy among the Greeks became far more widespread when they borrowed the alphabet from the Phoenicians. In about the fourteenth century B.C. the maritime city-states of Phoenicia had adapted the Sumerian "cuneiform" script to represent not syllables but something like the letters of the alphabet: later these letters were reduced from thirty-two to twenty-two. Semitic scripts were not strictly alphabetic, but rather a kind of shorthand: they were syllabic, but each syllable was represented by its initial element—though there were additional signs which added explicitness and could serve as vowels.

The Phoenician script may well have been ultimately based on the Egyptian hieroglyphics. Much the closest analogies to the earliest Greek inscriptions are found in the north-western parts of the Semitic world

Alphabet — script which systematically breaks the syllable into sonant and consonants

It seems to have been in about the eighth century B.C., when oriental influences were spreading, that certain Greeks adapted what they had learnt from the Phoenician traders and began to use a true alphabet in which vowels appeared regularly: that is to say they applied methodically, though with differing details in different regions, a device which the Semites had used irregularly and sporadically. At first the Greeks wrote from right to left, and then alternately in either direction (*boustrophedon*), and it was not until the fifth century B.C. that the left to right direction became universal.

"Boustrophedon" —like an ox ploughing

The adoption of the alphabet by the Greeks had a mighty liberating effect in the political, commercial and literary spheres. Literacy ceased to be the mysterious privilege of a specialised class.

⟨ 800–550 B.C. ⟩

Greek pastures
could support
sheep and goats
but not cattle.
With very little
hay, few large
animals could
be carried
through the
winter

Among Cumae's
settlers were
some of a small
tribe called
the "Graii" :
that is why the
Romans called
the Hellenes
"Graeci" and
why we call
them "Greeks"

In the eighth century began a large-scale wave of emigration from Greece. This was due to political struggles in this epoch of change ; to the Greek mainland's barren and irregularly watered soil, now inadequate to support an increasing population ; and to a new spirit of enterprise developed by the influx of oriental culture.

Trade, in the new expanding world, promoted the middle class. Colonisation was everywhere an expression of anti-aristocratic and anti-oligarchic feeling : though it was encouraged by the ruling classes as a salutary vent.

The first travellers left Greece on summer trading visits and piratical expeditions, and then —since the Phoenicians could no longer monopolise the seas—new cities were established abroad, from the Black Sea, Syria and Cyrenaica to France and Spain. The settlers brought with them their wives, families, gods and institutions, and became independent of their mother cities except in sentiment (sharing the same gods)—though Corinth later made an unusual attempt to reduce to dependent status the cities that it had founded.

The movement reached its climax towards the end of the seventh century, and then ceased when emergence of powers to east (Lydia, Assyria) and west (Etruria, Carthage) checked farther expansion. One of the most important regions in which new city-states were thus formed was Sicily and south Italy. The earliest of these western colonies (founded by Chalcis in Euboea) was Cyme (Cumae, c. 750), little more than 100 miles south of Rome and the principal source of its partial Hellenisation. Corinthians founded the great Sicilian state of Syracuse c. 734 B.C.

To begin with, the majority of emigrants came from the mainland, where conditions were most cramped. But in the seventh century there was a great burst of colonising activity by Ionian Miletus, now threatened by, and fortifying itself against, the Lydian kingdom in its hinterland : the mouths of the great Black Sea fishing rivers, the Danube, Dniester, Bug and Dnieper, were successively occupied by Milesian fishing and trading colonies.

Population was
increasing
through victories
by the city-states
over the
highlanders and
consequent
greater
expectation of
life

The settlements
are described as
"colonies"
though they were
independent

Naples—
Neapolis (the
new city)
Benghazi—
Pherenice
("victory-
bringer")
Monaco—
Monoecus (name
of Hercules)
Antibes—
Antipolis (the
city opposite)

Greek colonists
were on the Sea
of Marmora by
700 B.C., and
on the south
coast of the
Black Sea
before 600 B.C.

⟨ 750–600 B.C. ⟩

THE RULE OF LAW

"With written laws, the humblest in the state is sure of equal justice" —Euripides

New colonies had to have laws, for the law of the Greek states was the source of all standards of human life ; and these laws could now be written down, seen by all, and criticised if they seemed unsatisfactory. So the age of colonisation is also the age of the great lawgivers (though some of their names may reflect gradual codifications rather than the acts of single men).

Urukagina, King of Lagash, already tells of his efforts to relieve the misery of the very poor

An impressive legal system, strongly directed against extortion, had already appeared in the Sumerian state of Urukagina on the Persian Gulf (*c.* 2250 B.C.), and similar measures were incorporated in the Babylonian codification of Hammurabi (eighteenth century B.C.). But this, like the more developed Assyrian code which followed, was chiefly concerned with the law as a means of maintaining a just order.

In eighth-century Babylonia, when the discovery of cosmic periodicities led astronomers to regard the seven planets as the ultimate authority, god was evicted in favour of law. Then the Greeks, and the Persians too, fastened the law to an absolute standard of morality, thus setting it above the lawgiver. This is *Eunomia* : according to Hesiod, Justice and Peace "mind the works of men". This doctrine was the political creation of the aristocracies : it is a gospel of social discipline and service, in which responsibility was to correspond to privilege.

"Law is the king of all" —Pindar

A broken stone pillar at Chios (c. 600 B.C.) records a popular law court

The earliest known instance of such a Greek codification is traditionally attributed to Locri in south Italy ; its lawgiver Zaleucus (? *c.* 650 B.C.) was severe but sought to conciliate class rivalries (though Locri remained aristocratic).

Solon at Athens, appointed "archon and reconciler" to end civil strife, reformed the constitution on Eunomic lines. But though he reserved the chief offices for the nobility, he met the agitation of the rising middle class by defining the rights of the Assembly : the rights of all citizens to a share in the government, including some responsibility in the administration of justice, were secured.

"Though free, they are not absolutely free : for they have a master over them, the law"— Herodotus

Soon the Greeks employed the word isonomia, meaning an equal share of citizens in the laws (though not in property)

The Persians inherited from Babylon their consciousness of the "law which altereth not" (Daniel VI, 8, 12)

Solon revised the "draconic" code (introduced by Draco in 621 B.C.). Cases of homicide were early tried by the courts to minimise danger of blood feuds

⟨ **750–590 B.C.** ⟩

PERSONAL POETRY

The Iliad records that Agamemnon's mission found Achilles in his tent singing to his own accompaniment on the lyre

Instruction in singing and lyre-playing became part of the normal education of a Greek

Archilochus was a bastard, poor, and crossed in love. He says a man has wronged him

The introduction of the alphabet had encouraged the development of new sorts of literature, no longer based primarily on oral transmission. Then, during the seventh century B.C., great advances were made in Greek music. The climax of a number of discoveries was the establishment of a musical scale, which was thereupon fitted by Clonas to the flute and by Terpander of Lesbos to the lyre. This added greatly to the potentialities of the two principal Greek instruments, and enabled a poet to write songs knowing that they would be sung as he wished. The result was the creation of new sorts of poetry : the elegy and the lyric.

Greek music lacked harmony in the modern sense

The flute reached Greece from Babylonia via Asia Minor

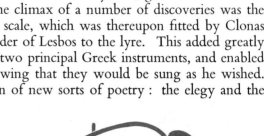

The personal elegy of the Ionian Archilochus of Paros was sung to the flute. Later, "elegy" meant love lament, but Archilochus, an original genius of great inventiveness, wrote and sang on many subjects—and reflected his own uncomfortable, wandering, frustrated life. This was a new individualistic kind of poetry. An individual was for the first time asserting moral responsibility and beginning to set his own beliefs and values against those generally accepted. Archilochus is far from completely subjective, but his likes and dislikes shine out with a clarity inconceivable in earlier traditions.

The elegiac couplet consists of the hexameter and pentameter (known to many children today from Ovid)

Individualistic lyrics of Asia Minor—"I hate a woman thick about the ankles" (Anon.) "There's nothing else that matters—only money" (Pythermus)

Sappho was small, dark and ugly. Wilamowitz surprisingly believed that she was "an excellent woman, wife and mother"

New techniques likewise developed rapidly among the first lyric poets, i.e. singers of poems to the lyre. Later in the seventh century, the Spartan Alcman wrote for choirs with fresh imagery, verbal music, and homely vivid phrase. This choral poetry found its chief home and inspiration in Dorian lands where the individual is less significant than his community. Monody, however, reached its climax on and off the coasts of Asia Minor where individualism was stronger ; and in the seventh and sixth centuries Alcaeus and Sappho introduced personal

poetry concerned with their own interests and emotions. Alcaeus was a violent defender of the landowning aristocracy against the tyrants ; Sappho writes of the loves and hatreds, the day-to-day pleasures and pains of a smart, idle society. Their contemporary Stesichorus, born in the west, wrote grand, dignified, lyrical narratives. So as not to offend Sparta, with which he formed a close connection, he offered a novel version of the Story of Helen, according to which the Helen who went to Troy was only a phantom.

Monody : lyric ode sung by single voice

Contemporary vase painters borrowed subjects from Stesichorus' poems

MIDDLE-CLASS ARMIES

The new mercantile class, created by much increased prosperity, urbanisation and civic development, supplied the new "hoplite" infantry which from the early seventh century B.C. began to replace the aristocratic cavalry as the basis of Greek armies. The idea of this heavily armed infantry seems to have come from the Levant, via Ionia. Their arms were costly, but they were numerous enough to overthrow constitutions.

The typical hoplite wore a helmet with nasal and cheek pieces, a breast-plate and bronze greaves, and carried a heavy, elliptical bronze shield, a short, straight, iron sword and a nine-foot-long spear. His charge was a quick march, and he was trained to manoeuvre and fight elbow to elbow.

A ninth-century-B.C. relief from the Turco-Syrian frontier shows a file of ten soldiers resembling hoplites

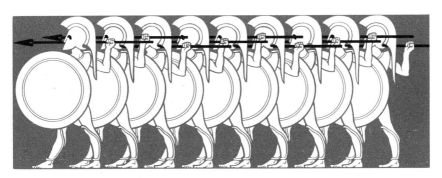

Light-armed troops in Greece were simply those who could not afford the heavy hoplite equipment

Hoplites were useless in rough country, and so much of Greece was rough. But the Greeks persevered with them and rarely experimented with light-armed guerrilla troops ; partly because of hoplite prestige won in the Persian wars, partly because of the political and social prestige of the class, and partly because of blind military conservatism.

⟨ **700–550 B.C.** ⟩

THE FIRST MONEY

An immense encouragement was given to the growth of trade by the development of coinage. Since the earliest times Egypt had regarded gold (found extensively in its territory) as the principal medium of exchange ; and the Sumerians had temple treasuries which became safe deposits and then banks. These and other peoples used rings, bars, ingots and lumps of metal for trading purposes. Iron "spits" were employed in some parts of Greece. True coinage was brought into existence by the Ionian Greeks and the wealthy non-Greek kingdom of Lydia in their hinterland. Many of the earliest coins are of white gold (electron) : the gold dust, mixed with silver, which was washed down from the hills within reach of both Ionia and Lydia. The first stage in the evolution of coinage was the incision of a punch mark ; then there were linear incisions. These marks may have guaranteed fineness or weight or both. At all events these early pieces circulated as bullion, not specie. Finally, on the model of stamped metal discs employed in Assyria and Syria, designs began to be cut into the surface, and intaglio dies were used (at first for one side only). These earliest seventh-century pieces were issued by merchants rather than by the state. The first incribed coin known to us, of Miletus or Ephesus, shows (beside a stag) the sentence, in Ionic Greek, "I am the sign (or badge) of Phanes". But civic and national devices soon appeared ; and coinage was now mature. We do not know how these discoveries were distributed between the Lydians and the Ionian Greeks. Possibly it was the Lydians who first punched and incised their pieces of metal, and the Ionians who first engraved designs on them. At any rate the Greeks were the only people who possessed both alphabetic writing and coined money.

The denomination name "drachma", still used, means—"a handful", i.e. originally of iron spits

"Coinage mature"—i.e., the pieces were :

1 intrinsically valuable

2 of deliberately adjusted weight

3 with the mark of a fully responsible authority

Near the end of the seventh century B.C. the custom of coinage came west across the Aegean. The primacy seems to belong to the island city of Aegina, with its famous "leather-backed turtles" ; before long came the "winged horses" of Corinth. At these cities there was good cheap export production. Greek cities were increasingly dependent on overseas trade for their foodstuffs : Aegina in particular was a small overpopulated island. Corinth, an active coloniser, used its colonies to increase trade.

The Athenian "owl" later became supreme

Turtle of Aegina   Winged horse of Corinth   Owl of Athens

THE TYRANTS

Qualifications for executive office, seats on Councils, votes in the Assembly, could now be calculated in money as well as land

12 per cent interest or more was charged for loans

Coinage revolutionised Greek society. It forced men to think quantitatively in many fields of life, and it advanced the middle classes at the expense of the aristocracies. Trade had been seriously hindered by the dangers of fraudulent bullion exchange. The farmer could now convert his surplus of produce into this medium of coinage, so easily reconvertible into any goods : and he could turn from subsistence to specialised farming and the export trade. The manufacturer could profitably make cheap goods, for the workman now had money to spend. But coinage also had grim results : cruel usury, mortgages and the enslavement of debtors.

The Greek city-states remained primitive in their attitude to banking : they never learnt or taught to stop hoarding bullion : money was never put out to breed

The prototype of the tyrants was Pheidon of Argos

This was the epoch of the brilliant, sophisticated Korai (female statues) at Athens and of the "black-figure" vase painting with a red background

City-states now began to be controlled by the rich as well as the aristocratic. But then, in the seventh century B.C., with the backing of the new hoplite middle class and the large, restive, city proletariats which they sought as allies, powerful individuals conducted *coups—*

Cleisthenes, tyrant of Sicyon (c. 600–570 B.C.) was violently anti-aristocratic

Pisistratus of Athens (560–527 B.C.) came into power by farcical tricks on popular emotion, including a bogus "Goddess Athena" to sponsor his coup. But he ruled successfully, encouraging the urban industrial population and small farmers

Cleisthenes, grandson of the tyrant of Sicyon, made the People's Assembly sovereign and wanted all citizens to have experience of government (508–7 B.C.)

taking advantage of some failure in foreign or internal policy—and ruled dictatorially as "tyrants". This particularly occurred in advanced areas, for example round the Corinthian isthmus, in Ionia, and (lasting longer) in Sicily. The tyrants were usually new-rich business men, mine-owners and financial speculators. They adopted imperialist foreign policies, and sought to relieve economic pressures by employing men on great public works and developing export industries. Poorer agricultural workers flocked in to share the benefits. But, harassed by exiled noblemen and the hostility of Sparta (and finally of the Delphic oracle too), the dynasties of tyrants rarely lasted for more than two generations. Then they succumbed either to the old governments by the few or—as at Athens under the statesman Cleisthenes—to more democratic régimes.

There were already hints in the Odyssey (and Hesiod) of a large "free" population earning a beggarly pittance by seasonal agricultural work

SPARTAN DISCIPLINE

It is disputed whether the helots were Dorians like the Spartans, or survivors of the pre-Dorian inhabitants

Dates attributed by the Greeks to Lycurgus ranged between 1100 and 600 B.C. Early archaeological finds show that a normal art at first existed

Sparta (Lacedaemon) did not develop like most other Greek city-states. The Spartans were a military aristocratic caste, living in a relatively large territory (3,200 square miles), among a population of subject peasant serfs (helots) who outnumbered them by at least seven to one. This circumstance was responsible for their peculiar way of life, attributed to the semi-legendary lawgiver Lycurgus. It may have assumed its characteristic features (after an earlier period of relative normality) during the seventh century B.C. The Spartan was subordinated to the community with exceptional rigour. He was not allowed to possess gold or silver; and Spartan art ceased. Education, daily life and marriage were all strictly and indeed ferociously regulated with a view to the maintenance of maximum military strength. Every citizen lived in a camp, under discipline, ready for instant action. Each year the government officially declared war anew on the helots ; and its secret police of young Spartans watched them incessantly and treated them ruthlessly. • Other Greeks did not imitate the Spartans, but many admired them, and they were the best soldiers in Greece.

Early Spartan history is largely patriotic fiction

Males received military instruction from the age of 7 to 30

Similar probouleutic Councils are found among the Germans of the first century A.D., and in mediaeval Novgorod

The Spartan constitution was a strange conglomeration of ancient hereditary collegiate kingship, five annual *ephors* ("overseers") chosen more or less by ballot, a Senate which included the kings and twenty-eight members appointed at an advanced age for the rest of their lives, and an Assembly which did not initiate its own business. In spite of this collection of survivals, the social changes of the seventh century are seen in a special feature of the Senate : this seems to have been the first Council in Greece to possess the function of *probouleusis*, i.e. of deciding on the measures to be deliberated in the Assembly. Probably this right—together with a new definition of the rights of the Assembly—was granted by the kings and ephors as a result of hoplite pressure. It enabled Sparta to incorporate the hoplites in the state without revolution.

The dual kingship has been conjecturally traced back to a prehistoric union of two villages

Athens, more democratic, provided a larger Council (500 by the end of the sixth century B.C.). It may have been elected by vote from the outset

The Spartan Assembly expressed its decisions not by voting but by shouting : the loudest shout prevailed

This ruthless minority régime at Sparta came to be regarded as the enemy of "democracy" and friend of those, in all cities, who hated it. Yet, by a curious paradox, it handed down to the Greek world not only the relatively democratic concept of *probouleusis* but ideas which were according to Greek theory even more democratic. For those few who possessed the hereditary franchise were equal *one with another*. Spartan equality in land ownership even inspired Athenian demands for a redistribution of land.

Helots, slaves and resident aliens, not being citizens, were irrelevant to "democracy"

ARCHAIC FRENZY

It was early believed that madness was of divine origin

There were similar epidemics of dancing in the Middle Ages and more recently

This was an age of unrest, ferment and fear of the supernatural—the age of the horribly exciting worship of Dionysus which had come to Greece early in the first millennium B.C. from Thrace, perhaps via Asia Minor. Reason did not prevail in archaic Greece. It was the home of semi-lunatic Sibyls, wandering shamans, ecstatic prophets and necromants, emotional mystic cults, grotesque myths, magic rituals and charms, miracle workers, mortifications, contagious religious frenzies and hysterical, orgiastic women. These flourishing survivals of remote antiquity were the signs and results of urgent psychological needs, of a prevalent guilt feeling, and of a fervent desire to break the bounds of narrow ancestral religion and to come nearer to the gods.

The prophets struck at the supremacy of their governments by claiming to receive divine revelation from the deity

Frenzied women pounced on animals or even children, tore them apart and ate them, as an act of communion with Dionysus

No precedents in other civilisations have been found for the promises of individual salvation to initiates

There were grim tales of posthumous punishments and purifications. There were also prospects of rewards in the after-life for initiates—the poor who had no rewards in this life were told to scorn it, and attach greater value to the life to come. Many such stories, and the tales of Hermes and the legendary Thracian singer Orpheus and their going down to the underworld, were written down and collected by sixth-century writers such as Onomacritus; literary form was thus given to all manner of crude popular beliefs.

All these beliefs and many more were summed up in "Orphic" literature

Of the many holy women in pathological trances the most influential was the Pythia at Delphi. The Delphic oracle, said to be at the navelstone of the earth, was of pre-Greek antiquity, but during the sixth century its priests set themselves to establish Apollo as the omniscient, authoritative moral councillor and imposer of law and order on the fevered Dionysiac hysteria of the earlier age: the new epoch needed ethical standards. From the seventh or sixth century a political league of northern and central states, earlier organised around a more northerly centre, became based on the Delphic cult which exercised a controlling influence.

Apollo was above all the god of purification; and purity was a matter of spirit as well as ritual

31

SEERS AND SCIENTISTS

In vigorous Ionia, early in the sixth century, progress took an epoch-making form under a group of versatile prodigies from Miletus (the leading Greek city of the day), who combined religious thinking with a new logical spirit as well as with a keen practicality. For the first time the human mind set itself to formulating a limited number of principles, and rigorously deducing truths from them. These men are sometimes called the first philosophers: they were also scientists, though with a certain over-logical disregard for the data of experience. Their brilliant brains were fertilised by the semi-technical literature of Egypt and Mesopotamia: it was their achievement to convert myths and lifeless priestly formulae into living thought. They proceeded on the entirely unproved assumption that the universe was an intelligible whole: they then applied to its major phenomena modes of thought derived from their control of techniques.

"Philosophia", at its highest, means an attempt to understand the world and mankind

The Greek word for universe, "kosmos", means order

Thales, who was reputedly half Phoenician, originated the science of metaphysics by suggesting that all material substances, however different they may seem to our senses, can really be reduced to one basic substance —and its pursuit has kept scientists busy ever since. Thales was the first Greek speculator to express his ideas in logical not mythological terms. His successor Anaximander (c. 546) conceived of the earth as in eternal motion, freely suspended in space (a great advance); he saw an ever-lasting balance of forces in nature, the Infinite, to which he ascribed a divine origin; and he speculated in a new scientific spirit on the origins of the human race. His younger contemporary Anaximenes, by his theory of condensation and rarefication, became the first to conceive the cosmos as governed according not to a moral but to a physical law.

Thales drew up an almanac and invented steering by the Pole Star instead of the Plough

Anaximander made the first map and regarded man as the product of natural evolution

Thales had travelled to Egypt and learnt Egyptian mathematics and Chaldean astronomy: he introduced to Greece, or invented, geometry. He also predicted within a year the solar eclipse of 585 B.C.

Anaximenes believed that the basic world substance was air (Thales had suggested water)

Pythagoras opposed Dionysiac frenzy with Apolline purity and legality. He also perhaps discovered "Pythagoras' Theorem"— though not in its Euclidean form—the square on the hypotenuse...

Far closer to the mysticism of the age than they, Pythagoras emigrated in c. 531 from Samos to Croton in south Italy, which he governed as the revered spiritual leader of a religious society: he believed in reincarnation, terminable by purity, and was held by Greeks to have introduced into philosophy the idea of a divine and immortal soul as opposed to the body. But he was also deeply interested in numbers: he discovered that the principal intervals of the musical scale correspond to certain arithmetical ratios between lengths of string at the same tension, the octave correspond-ing to the ratio 2 : 1, the fifth to 3 : 2 and the fourth to 4 : 3. This remarkable discovery led him to a numerical interpretation of the world as a whole.

PART THREE

500-336 B.C.

CLASSICAL GREECE

The *tempo* of events and thoughts accelerates still further, re-corded by amazingly numerous literary geniuses—a brief unity to repel Persian invasions—the Athenian League and its glory —the ruinous war between Athens and Sparta—Philip of Macedon ends the political power of the city-states for ever.

MARATHON

Darius' "Royal Road" from Susa to Sardis, over 1,500 miles long, stood at the centre of early Greek maps. It greatly extended geographical knowledge

When the Persians had conquered Croesus of Lydia (546 B.C.), they easily reduced, one after another, the Greek city-states on the western coasts of Asia Minor. Then the Persians turned eastwards and successively annexed Babylonia, the regions round the Aral Sea, and Egypt. Here was a new world power of unprecedented dimensions. The organisation of the Persian empire, a far more enlightened imperial system than had ever been known before, owed much to King Darius, who, after a period of disturbances, succeeded to the throne in 521 B.C.

These vast conquests were made by Cyrus I (558–528)

Darius took over the Lydian coinage and initiated a famous gold piece known as the "daric"

Darius crossed the Danube to intimidate the remote tribes beyond

Members of the Peloponnesian League were bound to Sparta (which crushed Argos in 494), not to each other

Darius secured his territories on the north side by the annexation of Thrace (c. 512). Twelve years later the Ionians rebelled under the leadership of Aristagoras of Miletus. They appealed for help to Sparta which had recently taken a significant and unusual step by uniting under her own control many cities in the permanent (offensive and defensive) Peloponnesian League, and was the strongest power in Greece. Sparta, however, refused to help, but Athens sent twenty ships (498) and the Euboean city Eretria also dispatched a contingent. Aristagoras sacked Sardis and created a fleet estimated at 353 ships, but Ionian morale was poor and Miletus fell to Persia (494). The revolt was at an end; and Persia's Phoenician navies replaced the Ionians in the Aegean. Darius now reorganised Greek Asia Minor, reconquered Thrace and planned to punish Athens and Eretria for helping the Ionians.

Athens was distressed at the failure of the revolt

The Athenian Assembly accepted the bold proposal of Miltiades to send the army to meet the Persians rather than await them outside unwalled Athens

Accompanied by the exiled Athenian dictator Hippias, a Persian expedition crossed the Aegean (reducing numerous islands), burnt Eretria, and landed their army in northern Attica, in the bay of Marathon. Athens raised 9,000 men under Callimachus (commander-in-chief for the year), advised by the experienced Miltiades. As the Persians began to march southwards along the coastal plain, the Athenians (supplemented by 1,000 men from Plataea) approached from the west and finally closed with them at a run (or quick march) and routed them. The survivors were picked up by ships. A large part of the Persian army, however, had not been engaged, and Athens was still threatened; the Persian fleet sailed right up to its harbour Phaleron. But then the Persians sailed away—the Athenian army from Marathon had returned, and a force of 2,000 Spartans, tardily dispatched, must have been close.

The Persians sent 600 ships under Datis and Darius' nephew Artaphernes

Estimated losses: Athenians—192 Persians—6400

Pheidippides: Sparta–Athens (150m.) in two days, returned, fought at Marathon, ran to Athens (26m.) to give news, dropped dead

BETWEEN THE INVASIONS

Though the Persians were unlikely to leave it at that, Athenian national morale and prestige had received infinite encouragement. During the next decade there were constitutional developments. So that the most competent war leaders could be chosen, the post of commander-in-chief appointed by lot was abolished—though, as a precaution against autocracy, the head of state (chief archon) was henceforward appointed by lot. At about the same time the curious and unfair institution of ostracism was introduced : every year the Assembly was asked whether it wished to ostracise anyone, and whoever received the largest adverse vote had to leave Attica for ten years. The intention was to protect the state against possible dictatorship, but owing to party disputes excellent statesmen were among the first to suffer. The survivor on the Athenian scene was Themistocles, whose determined policy it was to make Athens into a sea power, and in the 480s, after the Athenians had got the better of their maritime neighbours, their navy was greatly expanded.

After the unexpected rebuff to his commanders at Marathon, Darius determined upon early retribution. But Egypt revolted, and then the king died (485). His successor Xerxes, urged on by Greek exiles, decided in favour of a joint attack by sea and land. Xerxes and his army crossed the Hellespont (Dardanelles) by two bridges of boats and proceeded westward near the Thracian coast, accompanied by the fleet. The independence of Greece was directly threatened. Sparta and Athens combined to lead the resistance—Sparta as the greatest Greek power, and Athens as the victor of Marathon. A remarkable if short-lived phase of co-operation among the Greek states was initiated by their proclamation of a Hellenic congress at the Isthmus of Corinth. Under Spartan chairmanship, thirty-one city states vowed to resist, and to punish collaborators. Efforts were made to reconcile feuds, Athens sought internal unity by recalling her ostracised leaders, and it was agreed that Spartans should command both the army and the fleet.

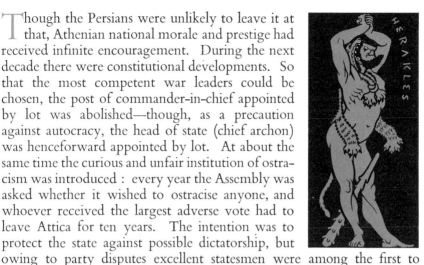

Some 25 years later, the artist Micon painted a great picture showing all the famous features of the battle, and the gods, goddesses and heroes who were held to have taken part in it

"Ostrakon"—a piece of crockery, placed in an urn after being inscribed with the name of the person whose ejection was desired

Already before Marathon, use had begun to be made of the large harbour of the Piraeus, better than exposed Phaleron

The Persian fleet included Egyptians, Phoenicians, peoples of Asia Minor—including subject Greeks

The Persian army perhaps amounted to 180,000 men of 46 nations. To keep touch with the fleet, a canal 1½ miles long was dug across the Isthmus of Mt. Athos

The general was King Leonidas and the admiral was Eurybiadas

Athens, finding allied opinion against her, withdrew her claim to the naval command

⟨ 490—480 B.C. ⟩

THERMOPYLAE

Troops were sent to Tempe but were withdrawn when it became clear that the pass could be turned

The northern Greeks had tried to commit themselves to neither side, but the Thessalians urged the confederates to send troops for the defence of the pass of Tempe. It was planned to defend Thermopylae instead—eighty miles south, a narrow pass between mountains and sea—and every Greek state north of it submitted to Persia. Leonidas marched to Thermopylae with about 7,000 men, including only 300 Spartans; more were alleged to follow after a religious festival, but it is likely that the Spartans were unwilling to commit many troops north of the Isthmus, though compelled to make a show of doing so for fear of losing the support of Athens and its fleet.

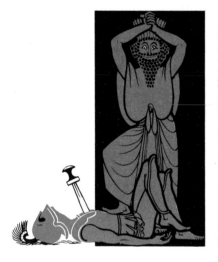

In July 480 the Persian army reached Thermopylae and the Persian navy the Thessalian coast to its north-east. The Greek fleet off northern Euboea (Artemisium) was helped by storms to fight an indecisive campaign. On land there was a fierce clash in which Greek spearmen had the better of Persian bowmen. But then a Persian élite force guided by a Greek turned Thermopylae by a mountain path; most of the defenders retreated south leaving Leonidas with 1,400 men (Spartans, Thebans and Thespians) in the pass, where they were annihilated. Several thousand other Greeks also fell, and the remnants of the Greek force fell back through Boeotia. The Thebans and most other Boeotians submitted to Persia.

The Greek fleet numbered 333 ships, including 200 Athenian vessels

The retreat was perhaps in hope of surrounding the Persian column

A column was erected at Sparta with the names of Leonidas and his 300 Spartans

When the Greek fleet off Artemisium heard the news of Thermopylae, it sailed down the Euripus (the channel between Euboea and the mainland) to the coast of Attica—only to find that the main body of the Spartan and Peloponnesian army, having begun to move once the festival was over, instead of advancing into Boeotia as had been planned had stopped short at the Isthmus and was fortifying it. So Themistocles and the Athenians decided to evacuate Athens, and conveyed most of its men, and its women and children, to places of safety, leaving only a small garrison on the Acropolis. Meanwhile the allied fleet stood in the bay of the neighbouring island of Salamis. Xerxes occupied Athens, took and burnt the Acropolis, and his fleet sailed into Phaleron.

The Acropolis garrison resisted for a fortnight

The Greek fleet lay in the narrow sound between the island of Salamis and the mainland

The Peloponnesians wanted to withdraw their fleet to the Isthmus and await the Persians there, but Themistocles, by threatening Athenian mass-withdrawal to Sicily or Italy, persuaded them to fight off Salamis. In these narrow waters (at one point only a mile wide) after a day of confused, crowded fighting the Persian navy was utterly defeated.

Now 385 ships

⟨ 480 B.C. ⟩

PERSIAN WITHDRAWAL

Themistocles, though of dubious public morals, was a strategic genius whose naval policy accelerated Athenian democracy

Xerxes, fearing that the news of Salamis would provoke an Ionian revolt, marched with 60,000 men back to the Dardanelles, sending the surviving portion of his fleet to secure his crossing. The bridge had gone, but Themistocles now failed to persuade the Greek admirals to strike at the Dardanelles, and Xerxes crossed by ship and proceeded to Sardis. The Greek commanders met at the Isthmus to distribute the plunder, and the battle was commemorated by the leading poets and artists of the day. It greatly developed the idea of Hellenism—of Greeks as opposed to barbarians—and it was widely felt to be a worthy sequel to that legendary victory of west over east, the Trojan War. But as in all Greek wars for centuries to come, the decision had been reached on the sea.

Themistocles by a trick had persuaded the Persian fleet to attack when its forces were divided

Greek religion gained in intensity from the battle—"It is not we who have done this!" said Themistocles, "It is the gods and heroes"

The intrusive channels of Greek seas gave the naval arm a unique reach

The main body of the Persian army withdrew to Thessaly under Mardonius, who was joined in the following spring by Xerxes' escort : his total force may have numbered 120,000. The Greeks were still in the gravest danger, since they were disunited—the Spartans refused to fight in northern Greece—and they lacked cavalry. The Persian fleet, however, was absent, for it had to guard Ionia. Mardonius advanced, and the Athenians evacuated their city again, but still rejected Persian proposals. Finally Sparta agreed to send a force into Attica, and a combined army not far short of 100,000 men under the Spartan regent Pausanias confronted the Persians near Plataea (August 479). The hoplite spearmen routed the Persians and killed their commander. The Persian survivors fled, including a considerable force that had not fought ; the threat to Greece was at an end. It was largely a Spartan victory—the Athenians had little to do with it. But a few days later the Greek fleet, including many Athenian ships, landed a force in Ionia, near Cape Mycale, and sacked the enemy camp ; whereupon the Ionians deserted the Persians and asserted their freedom. The Spartans returned home, but the Athenian and Ionian navies proceeded to the Dardanelles and took its strongest fortress, Sestos.

"So long as the sun moves in his present course, we shall never come to terms with Xerxes" (Athens)

Mardonius made overtures to Athens. The Spartans still remained behind the Isthmus

This is the event with which Herodotus of Halicarnassus (S.W. Asia Minor) the world's first great historian (484–? 424 B.C.) ends his account of the Persian War

⟨ 480–479 B.C. ⟩

SICILY

The autocratic luxury and grandeur of Syracuse is commemorated by the most sublime of lyric poets—Pindar of Thebes

It was believed that messages were exchanged between the Persians and the Carthaginians, via the Phoenicians

Outstandingly fertile among Greek lands is Sicily; and there, too, at the time of the Persian invasions of Greece, western Hellenism had to face its decisive threat, from the Carthaginians. Carthage had succeeded Sidon and Tyre as the greatest Phoenician maritime power, and it had established harbour-cities in western Sicily, from which it maintained contact with settlements on the coast of Sardinia (rich in corn and metals), and planned to suppress the Greek states in the rest of Sicily. Probably its attack on these was deliberately timed to coincide with the campaigns of Xerxes on the Greek mainland, so that no reinforcements could pass from one group to Greek states of the other.

Carthage was founded by settlers from Tyre, c. 814 B.C.

Greek Sicily was dominated by four dictators: there was a family group in the north—Anaxilas at Messina (who controlled both sides of the strait), and his father-in-law Terillus at Himera; and a family group in the south—Gelon of Syracuse, now becoming a great naval power, and his father-in-law Theron of Acragas, a city now second only to Syracuse in wealth and strength. Carthage had her chance when Theron attacked and expelled Terillus: for his son-in-law Anaxilas then appealed to the Carthaginians. A large Carthaginian force under Hamilcar landed at Panormus (Palermo) and marched along the coast to Himera, where after a long and desperate battle it was annihilated and Hamilcar was killed by the joint armies of Theron and Gelon (480). Six years later,

Popular fancy believed that Himera and Salamis were fought on the same day

Gelon's brother and successor Hieron fought off the other menace to western Hellenism, the Etruscans whose twelve city-states controlled a great area of central Italy and had, with Carthage, inflicted a shattering defeat on Greek navies off Corsica (c. 535). The northernmost Greek colony in Italy, Cyme (Cumae), had checked Etruscan southward expansion and Rome had risen and expelled its Etruscan kings. Then, in 474, an Etruscan naval expedition against Cyme was decisively defeated by Hieron's Syracusan fleet, and the Etruscans were never again a serious threat to the western Greeks. The latter, under the democracies to which the dictators soon gave place, attained increasingly spectacular, though sometimes vulgar and frivolous, prosperity.

Hieron's despotic rule was enforced by a large secret police system

After the fall of the tyrants Ducetius tried but failed to assert the native population against the Sicilian Greeks

The expulsion of the Tarquins from Rome was followed by a further setback for the Etruscans when they were defeated by the Latins at Aricia

THE ATHENIAN EMPIRE

There were ultimately about 200 allies of Athens

Contributions were according to means: tactfully assessed by Aristides

In the forty years after Plataea, Athens increased its allies and formed them first into the voluntary League of Delos, with anti-Persian objectives, and then into an empire. The members of the League contributed ships or money. Most preferred money contributions, but Athens preferred them to give ships, which she herself controlled and manned (thus mitigating Athenian unemployment). Athens and her port, the Piraeus, were joined by Long Walls, their fortifications completed, and their devastated houses rebuilt.

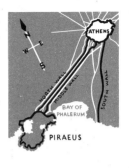

MILES

The League's treasury was established at Delos, the ancient centre of Ionian worship

Though Pericles was retiring and intellectual, his oratory gained him repeated annual re-elections to one of the ten policy-making generalships

Soon cities were coerced to join the Delian League and rebellious members were reduced by force (Naxos and Thasos). Increasingly the League assumed imperial form, with compulsory military service, dictated constitutions and growing Athenian jurisdiction. Force became more and more often necessary, as Greek sentiment resented any least derogation of autonomy.

Themistocles was ostracised c. 472 and succeeded by the pro-Spartan aristocrat Cimon, who was discredited when he was snubbed by Sparta (462)

With Pericles' rise to power in Athens, the ancient Council of the Areopagus was stripped of most powers; the archonship (p. 20) was made a paid office open to the middle class, and judges too were paid. This Athenian democracy was conducted by an Assembly where every *citizen* could attend, speak and initiate motions. So Equity, or the Will of the People, dethroned Law as the ultimate sanction: the grave danger of irresponsibility was countered by the increasedly important Council (Boule) of 500 which filtered business for Assembly consideration (p. 30).

The total number of voters was perhaps 40,000; this was direct not representative government

The Boule's constantly changing membership prevented it from dominating the government

Guided by Pericles, the Spartan alliance was abandoned and an aggressive imperialism attempted on many fronts: there was even an unsuccessful expedition against Persian-controlled Egypt. Athens subjected Aegina and established control at Megara and in Boeotia. Expenditure had been enormous, and Athens negotiated a "Five Years' Truce" with Sparta and attempted unsuccessfully to summon a Panhellenic Congress (c. 449).

Cimon was recalled from ostracism after the truce

The citizens of the cleruchies were mainly Athenian unemployed, and retained their status as Athenians

Athens imported from afar grain, wheat, flour, nuts, meat, cheese, sails, wood, incense, carpets, ivory

But Pericles, aiming to extend the Athenian empire at the expense of the other Greeks, made peace with Persia (c. 448). Athens then lost her continental possessions, but established a new type of subject settlement (cleruchy) in Euboea, other islands and the Dardanelles. The use of Athenian coinage, weights and measures was enforced throughout most of the empire. Athens caused resentment by building herself ships from League resources, but further revolts were crushed. Pericles fostered relations with the western Greeks and the vital corn-producing Black Sea area to support Athens' huge excess population.

The Athenian population of about 310,000 was more than four times greater than the state's own food resources could support

⟨ 479–431 B.C. ⟩

SPLENDOUR AND SLAVERY

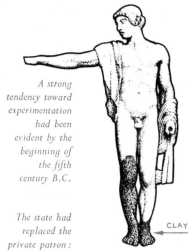

CLAY

After the Persian wars Greek art had developed the features of truly classical Hellenism. The old sense of decoration remained but was firmly controlled, and there prevailed an austere simplicity and a severe, elevated spirit of idealism. Sculpture played a prominent part in this full, conscious flowering of humanism which is our most encouraging heritage from the fifth century. The thirty years after the war saw the production of some of the greatest masterpieces of Greek stone-carving, culminating in the pediment of the temple of Zeus at Olympia (dedicated 456) with its noble figure of Apollo. At this time too the red-figure pictures and vases of Polygnotus were showing "men better than ourselves".

Imperial Athens possessed the desire and the resources to employ the greatest artists of this uniquely artistic age. She used the contributions of her allies not only to build her navy, but to reconstruct her streets—which were narrow, dirty, ill-paved and badly lit—and, with the utmost magnificence, her temples, destroyed by the Persians. The classical balance, purity and moderation appear in the new temple of Athena (designed by Ictinus on the rebuilt Acropolis), the Parthenon. Its Doric architecture, in smooth-grained marble from Mount Pentelicon, reveals great mathematical subtlety, and the sculptured reliefs display a sophisticated fluency far in advance of the Apollo of Olympia. League money was also spent on extensive social constructions at Athens: for example, the baths and athletic institutions which played so large a part in the education of its citizens.

Whether women were allowed much enjoyment of Athenian amenities is often disputed; they must have spent a good deal of time in their small, dark, insanitary houses. It is beyond dispute, however, that the Athenian economy was based on slavery, which had increased rapidly from about 600 B.C.—when cities developed industry and the demand for workmen outran the supply of free labour. Theorists, and kindly people, were constantly worried by the dilemma implicit in the fact that the slave was a chattel and yet a human being. Awkward questions were raised by the enslavement of Greek citizens during the Peloponnesian War, but it was not until the following century that liberal opinion increasingly dwelt on the human rights of slaves.

FIFTH-CENTURY THOUGHT

Heraclitus, like Pythagoras, was recognised as a prophet

Logos : word = truth of Universe

Empedocles produced the theory of breathing through the pores as well as the nose and mouth. He also led a democratic revolution in Sicily

During the fifth century B.C. Greek philosophy and science made unprecedented strides. Heraclitus, writing at the turn of the century, was the first seer and thinker concerned with the nature of knowledge and the human soul—the first mental philosopher : exerting an enormous influence on Socrates, the Stoics and the future. He stressed the *Logos*, of which the chief content was the basic unity of things (eternal Justice) underlying the apparent oppositions which exist in a state of strife. He compared this unity to the attunement of opposite tensions in the bow and the lyre. The world substratum (= the Infinite of the earlier Ionians) is Fire, identified by its unifying and directive capacity with the *Logos*.

Parmenides rejected earlier theories of the diversity of nature ("mere evidence of the senses and so delusion") and saw the universe as single, immobile, spherical, without beginning or end. Empedocles refused to believe in this unity or absence of movement. He interpreted the universe instead as a spherical plenum in which Love (attraction) and Strife (repulsion) alternately predominate. Anaxagoras envisaged a spherical universe which was composite, including the "seeds" (forerunners of Atoms) of flesh, blood, bone, gold and other natural substances—"a multitude of innumerable seeds in no way like each other". Leucippus originated the materialistic Theory of Atoms, and maintained that the final principles are : (1) atoms—innumerable, tiny, variously-shaped, solid particles colliding and agglomerating ; and (2) empty space—void but extant. Democritus elaborated Leucippus' atomic theory, and also contributed to a rising cosmopolitan spirit—"the native land of a good soul is the whole universe".

Heraclitus pointed out that human values are not absolutely valid. "Fools when they hear are like the deaf" "God is day and night, winter and summer, war and peace, surfeit and hunger"

Parmenides' cosmology was, perhaps for the first time, non-mythical— a historical description

Anaxagoras went to Athens in c. 462 B.C., and did much to transplant Ionian philosophy there. He believed that the heavenly bodies were thrown off from initially revolving matter by centrifugal force

Alongside their concern with such ultimate problems, these and other philosophers produced a great volume of knowledge in other fields—in Physics, Logic, Psychology, Poetry, Music, Mathematics, Astronomy, Technology, etc. At this time also flourished the most famous of physicians, Hippocrates of Cos, though it was disputed even in antiquity which books of the "Hippocratic Corpus" were his work. Plato ascribes to him a body of doctrine and the belief that human bodies are naturally healthy and tend to recover.

⟨ **500—400 B.C.** ⟩

HEROIC TRAGEDY

Satyric plays dealt grotesquely with ancient legends, the chorus dressed to represent satyrs, with horses' tails or goats' legs

Aristotle regards the choral dithyramb as another ancestor of tragedy. Archilochus called dithyramb the Song of Dionysus and claimed to lead others in singing it while his wits were thunderstruck with wine

Aeschylus, c. 525–456 B.C., surviving plays: ''Suppliants'' ''Persians'' ''Seven Against Thebes'' ''Oresteia Trilogy'' (Agamemnon, Libation Bearers, Eumenides) ''Prometheus Bound''

At the Athenian spring festival of Dionysus Eleuthereus, the festival of the Great Dionysia, three poets competed each year, each presenting three tragedies and a "satyric" play. Tragic drama apparently originated from religious rites of a dramatic character ; it was said by Aristotle to have developed from the "satyric" plays, of which we see the characters, gradually becoming less caricaturish, on sixth-century black-figure vases. These "goat-singers" were revolutionised by Thespis (prize winner for tragedy at Athens in 534), who was the first to appear as an actor separate from the chorus. He spoke a prologue and set speeches which introduced a new intensity of dramatic action and feeling. The great days of Attic tragedy extended between Aeschylus' first victory in 484 and the deaths of Sophocles and Euripides in c. 406.

goat-singers = tragodoi

Greek tragedy is often concerned with two ideas : *hubris* and *nemesis*. *Hubris* is presumptuous conduct or speech : *nemesis* is the anger or dislike which such conduct or speech provokes ; presumption arouses anger and merits punishment. These conceptions agreed with the idea of just, inevitable retribution, which was already familiar in Greece long before the fifth century. (Retributive justice in politics assumed the significance of equalising, levelling—and played a large part in the rise of democracies.)

The chorus sang reflections on the dramatic action

"Know yourself"—know that you are human—was the enduring lesson, and it raised inescapable questions concerning man's relations with the deity. Aeschylus, profoundly religious, links Fate with the gods and with Zeus, who is omnipotent and righteous. Sophocles depicts the horrifying downfall of Oedipus as the most striking illustration of human powerlessness in the face of god-sent fate. In the most complicated and apparently fortuitous series of happenings there is a design, though we cannot tell what it means. Yet for Sophocles, religion though piously revered is the framework of his primary dramatic concern—the doings, sufferings and feelings of mankind. In Aeschylean tragedy the interest had concentrated on action, and on subordination to the gods, less than on human psychology. Sophocles introduced purely human drama, combining forceful complex personalities.

The flexible, rich clarity of the Greek language had reached its zenith

Sophocles, c. 496–406 B.C., surviving plays: ''Ajax'' ''Antigone'' ''Oedipus the King'' ''Trachinian Maidens'' ''Electra'' ''Philoctetes'' ''Oedipus at Colonus''

THE SOPHISTS

The word *sophistes* first appears in the fifth century B.C., meaning a skilled or wise man; then it came to be applied to the profession of itinerant teachers who preached self-help from town to town. Before long the Sophists, with their emphasis on success and agile argument, came to be regarded as sceptics. Plato was shocked by suggestions that the State was *conventional* (as opposed to natural), and he blamed the individualism of his day on a sophistic saying *might is right*.

Gorgias wrote that nothing exists; that if anything exists it is unknowable; and that if anything can be known, language cannot communicate the knowledge. He won great fame at Athens for his public speaking, and by preaching the unity of Greece during the Peloponnesian war he contributed greatly to the spread of Panhellenism. Protagoras claimed to teach efficient living (*arete*). He announced that "man is the measure of all things", i.e. all views and qualities are relative (noblemen owe their superiority to longer schooling); no science is universally valid, but man can master his environment by superior rational knowledge; and no certainty can be expressed about the existence of the gods. But he urged that men should obey the moral codes of their cities. His main contribution was to advance the view that man is a social animal whose implanted social instincts (creating institutions and conventions) raise him above the brutes and make communities possible. Hippias described law as the "tyrant of mankind", the bond of humanity as stronger than that of nationhood, and all wise men, of whatever country, as fellow-citizens by nature: thus he laid the foundations of cosmopolitanism and prepared the way for an entirely new view of slavery. Critias wrote a rationalist account of the gods: he called them a cunning invention by rulers in case law missed a crime. Antiphon seems to have regarded the ordinary man's standards as arbitrary and unnatural; he also held that Greeks did not possess better natural gifts than barbarians, and that inequality of wealth was a prime cause of dissension. Thrasymachus is famous for his defence (in Plato's *Republic*) of the opinion that justice is the interest of the stronger. Lycophron was one of the first to put forward the theory that the State should be an instrument for protection against injustice. He is sometimes regarded as the founder of the Doctrine of Contract.

⟨ 450–400 B.C. ⟩

THE PELOPONNESIAN WAR

At the beginning of the war the Athenians under Pericles withdrew into their Long Walls—to take refuge from annual Spartan invasions—and raided Spartan territory from the sea. But a plague in the crowded town was disastrous to this policy. Pericles died in disfavour in 429

Athens scored a great prestige success in 425 by capturing 292 of the almost mythical Spartan hoplites at Sphacteria (west coast of the Peloponnese)

Alcibiades' clever offensives were frustrated by the suspicions he roused in Athens. In 415–12 he deserted to the enemy

The imperial and commercial achievements of Athenian sea-power had earlier involved her in hostilities with the land-power Sparta, and in 431 B.C. began a period of twenty-seven years in which the two cities were generally at war. This Peloponnesian War (as it is called from the Athenian point of view) ranged the peoples of Greece in two groups. Athens had her empire and its tribute, a few other scattered allies, and her powerful fleet. Sparta, with less funds, controlled the greater part of the Peloponnese, the Isthmus including Athens' naval and commercial rival Corinth, and central Greece including Boeotia, where Thebes effectively supplemented Sparta's own unrivalled hoplite force. Athens had to use her sea-power at the periphery of the Spartan alliance, where naval superiority had a chance to detach its members. The Spartans employed their land-power to invade Attica itself and Thrace. Operations were often insignificant, but the war is eternally memorable because of the outstanding Athenian historian Thucydides, scientifically concerned with the laws of human nature in politics, who extracted permanently valuable political lessons from the decline and fall of the geographically small but exceptionally illuminating Athenian empire.

Success in the long, intermittent war swung to and fro, with Athens several times within an ace of final victory—under "the people's watch-dog" Cleon and the brilliant, amoral Alcibiades—and several times heavily defeated, as in the catastrophic expedition against Sicily, which was almost completely annihilated. Yet the progress of hostilities witnessed the gradual exhaustion of Athens' financial and naval resources. She ceased to compete with her opponents when Persia brought her wealth into the balance on the side of Sparta, and in 405 B.C., at Aegospotami on the Dardanelles, Athens lost her last fleet. Athens itself fell to siege by starvation in 404. Through incompetence, hysteria and intrigues among her leaders she had lost the war, her fortifications and all her foreign possessions. Her political pre-eminence was over. Apart from Thucydides, that is the main importance of the war in world history—and Sparta was the unchallengeable supreme power in Greece.

Corinth brought in Sparta to counter Athenian support of Corinth's disloyal colony Corcyra. Athens was embarrassed by a revolt of her dependent Potidaea in Macedonia

Thucydides describes, with exceptional power, the appallingly violent class-warfare initiated by Corcyra in 427–5, and the catastrophic Athenian expedition against Syracuse in Sicily (415–13)

After the Sicilian defeat, Athens' allies deserted her and there was a short-lived right-wing coup

The Persian prince Cyrus helped the Spartan Lysander to capture Ionia and the Dardanelles (408–7)

The oligarchy of the Thirty Tyrants was established in Athens, and Alcibiades was assassinated in exile (404)

Athens was allowed to remain independent herself, but the Long Walls were pulled down to the merry sound of flutes

NEMESIS

NEW DRAMA

Euripides
c. 480–406.
Surviving plays:
"Children of
Heracles"
"Alcestis" (438)
"Medea" (431)
"Hippolytus"
(428)
"Hecuba"
"Suppliants"
"Andromache"
"Madness of
Heracles"
"Trojan
Women" (415)
"Electra"
"Iphigenia in
Tauris"
"Helen"
"Phoenician
Maidens"
"Seven Against
Thebes"
"Orestes" (408)
"Bacchants"
"Rhesus"

Athenian prisoners at Syracuse were said to have won their freedom by being able to recite Euripides

The Peloponnesian War moulded the plays of the last great tragedian, Euripides, and the greatest of comic dramatists, Aristophanes. Euripides, born (it was said) on the day of Salamis, wrote eighty or ninety plays, won the prize only five times, and emigrated to Macedonia in 408. His subjects were violent, stressful and fraught with passionate conflicts: he frequently horrified his contemporaries by implied sceptical criticism of traditional morality and religion. His victimised, doomed, morbid, noble or distraught men or (more often) women are depicted with new insight. Loving heroism and nature, and writing with a deep and truthful sympathy, he nevertheless found human existence—and the Greece of the Peloponnesian War—bitter and disillusioning. Though nearer to life than Aeschylus and Sophocles, he preferred to display that life within a formal framework of dramatic devices such as the prologue, "recognition" and *deus ex machina*. The choral passages of his plays include many moving lyrics, and his style is limpid and readily adapted to deep feeling.

Recognition: revelation at critical moment of unsuspected relationship

Athenian Old Comedy is a combination of many elements derived from earlier culture—Dorian "episodes", the Dionysiac revel at Athens (*Komos*), antique fairy stories, Ionian humorous tales, traditional ferocity and obscenity. These very dissimilar elements were welded into a dramatic form of which the supreme master is Aristophanes, a comic playwright of genius. His staunch, "commonsense", conservative political views led him to astonishingly outspoken pacifism during the war itself, from which the common man of the country party (for whom he speaks) was the worst sufferer. His eye was keenly directed towards the absurdities in all current opinions, customs and controversies. The basic subject matter of Old Comedy is personal abuse, usually directed against notorious politicians. Innovations in literature, music, religion and society displeased Aristophanes. In comic situation, farce, parody and satire he is unequalled, and his choric odes are lovely poems.

The provider of a victorious tragic or comic chorus was crowned and rewarded with a bronze tripod

Aristophanes,
c. 448–c. 380,
surviving plays:
"Acharnians"
(425)
"Knights"
(424) .
"Clouds" (423)
"Wasps" (422)
"Peace" (421)
"Birds" (414)
"Lysistrata"
(411)
"Thesmophoria-
zusae" (410 or
411) "Frogs"
(405) "Ecclesia-
zusae" (392)
"Plutus" (388)

Aristophanes' choruses are usually animals, women, foreigners or abstractions

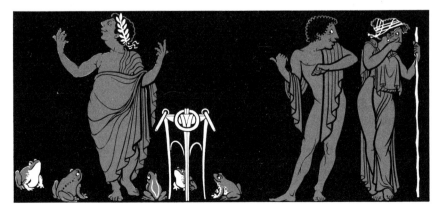

⟨ 438–388 B.C. ⟩

THE SOUL AND THE STATE

More or less faithful accounts of Socrates' teaching appear in several authors as well as Plato

"The man who is master of himself is truly free"

A contributory reason for Socrates' condemnation was his friendship with enemies of the democracy which soon succeeded the Thirty Tyrants (403 B.C.)

Socrates of Athens, 469–399 B.C., left nothing in writing ; but he gave a decisive turn to human thought. Before him cosmology had been the main interest of philosophic speculation, after him it was human conduct. He seems to have been the first to apply serious critical and philosophic thought to questions of personal conduct, and the first to emphasise the necessity of systematic definition of the terms used in such discussions. So he exercised a decisive influence on the future of logic as well as of moral philosophy. The main doctrine to which he tends is *virtue is knowledge* (i.e. usually knowledge of the individual's happiness or good). His custom of teaching the younger generation in conversation, questioning institutions and motives—including certain traditional beliefs, although Socrates was deeply religious and opposed to Sophistic scepticism—was made the subject of a trumped-up charge resulting in his condemnation and execution.

Aristotle, Xenophon and Plato agree in attributing to Socrates inductive arguments and general definitions

Socrates was humorous, brave, indifferent to comfort and untiring in conversation

Plato attacked art as mere imitation of nature. Contemporary sculpture displayed a more human conception of the gods ; e.g. in the technically superlative Hermes of Praxiteles, and in Scopas' free emotional sculptures at Tegea

The fame of Plato (*c.* 427–347 B.C.) is based on his twenty-five superbly written dialogues, and on the *Letters* (not all genuine). Socrates was his inspiration and bequeathed to him the conviction that the proper study of mankind is Man's Ultimate Good. After about fourteen years of travelling Plato returned to Athens and founded his Academy, where he taught for nearly forty years. In his *Republic* Plato outlines his Utopian city-state, slave-owning, class-divided and chauvinistic, based on the view that government is an exact science requiring expert knowledge and masterable only by a few in each generation. This opinion impels him to condemn democracy, though his racially pure elite are to live communistic lives. Plato favoured censorship, conscription, state education and state control of economic and social life and of individual thought. In his *Laws* he reiterates the theoretical perfection of communist unity, but favours in practice a "mixed constitution", avoiding extremes of poverty and wealth. The ideal state will be largely ruled by law (earlier regarded as second best to governmental skill) and religion (earlier rated subordinate to dialectic) ; and it will contain only 5,040 male citizens—so Plato's viewpoint is bounded by the classic, small, unco-operative Greek city-state.

Plato's "Phaedo" contains a description of Socrates' last hours, and his Doctrine of Forms—which implies immortality of the soul

Plato's last period produced technical studies of perception and knowledge, metaphysics and natural science

His "Statesman" suggests that the ideal ruler should be hampered neither by people nor constitution

Lysander brought
a Persian
testimonial back
to Sparta, but
when opened
it proved to
be abusive

The single defeat
at Cnidus was
enough to ruin
Sparta's
precarious
sea power

B y her victory, Sparta was drawn into founding an empire. Her supremacy in Greece lasted for thirty years. But it was crudely exercised and incomplete, she was unfit for it, and she owed its maintenance to Persia, which dictated the King's Peace (387–6). Persia retained Ionia, but Athens had begun to show her recovery when she rebuilt her Long Walls (by Persian permission) and Conon (as Persian admiral) defeated the Spartans at Cnidus (394). Sparta then broke down the significant Olynthian confederacy formed in Macedonia (379) —claiming that it infringed the independence of cities proclaimed by the Peace—but *en route* broke the Peace herself by seizing Thebes (382), which freed itself. Soon afterwards a Spartan governor attempted a similar *coup* at the Piraeus (379–8) : Athens and Thebes became allies, and Athens was again at war with Sparta.

Persia suffered a
loss of prestige
when a Greek
mercenary force
supporting Cyrus
against his
brother
Artaxerxes
penetrated as far
as Babylonia.
Xenophon's
"Anabasis"
records their
dramatic
vicissitudes

Renewed
Athenian
imperialism
caused fatal
revolts (from
357)

Athens now attempted to form a Second Athenian League, of defensive character and ostensibly less tyrannical than the first. After Thebes repelled Spartan invasions and Athens defeated Spartan navies, Athens took the initiative in the Peace of Callias (371) by which she and Sparta recognised each other's zones of influence. Sparta's attempt at domination was at an end, and her rapid decline was soon to follow.

The new
Athenian League
was bi-cameral :
there was an
Assembly of the
Confederates
parallel to the
Athenian
Assembly

Athenians
laughed at the
Boeotians as
stodgy,
inartistic
agriculturalists

The Peace confirmed the independence of Greek states, but Thebes maintained that her supremacy over Boeotian cities was justified since Boeotia was a geographical unit like Attica. This was arguable, though the Boeotian situation was different : for three-quarters of a century, since 447, the country had been organised as a League of cities, remarkable as a pioneer of federal government and as a pioneer—in this Greek world of primary Assemblies—of a thoroughgoing representative system. But Thebes had never been able to assert herself as a Greek power. Now, however, under Pelopidas and the military genius Epaminondas, Thebes took the centre of the Greek scene after her epoch-making defeat of the Spartans at Leuctra (371). Thebes then invaded the Peloponnese several times, encouraged a new league of all Arcadian cities, created a new land power even closer to Sparta— in Messenia—and threatened Sparta itself. But Theban expansion did not survive the death of Pelopidas (364), and of Epaminondas during a fourth invasion of the Peloponnese (battle of Mantinea, 362).

There was no
primary Assembly
at Boeotia : the
cities each sent
delegates to a
federal council
of 600, of
which each
quarter in turn
acted as a
preparatory
committee. But
Thebes had
always tended
to dominate
this league

Pelopidas was
killed fighting
Alexander of
Pherae at
Cynoscephalae

Theban success
was largely due
to the Sacred
Band of 150
pairs of personal
friends

IMPERIALISM IN SICILY

Dorians and Ionians in Sicily were sharply divided, and non-Greeks keen to profit from their strife

Syracuse had been so weakened by repelling the Athenian invasion (415–13) that for some time she was unable to assert herself against other Sicilian city-states, or against the Carthaginians who avenged their defeat at Himera—seventy-one years earlier—by destroying that and other cities.

Dionysius I employed the natives as mercenaries

The Carthaginian capture of Acragas (406) caused a revolution at Syracuse, where Dionysius I, the Machiavellian, ruthless son of a mule-driver, seized autocratic power and retained it for nearly forty years by technical military improvements (e.g. in siege craft), by sea power, and by savage oppression (concealed by outward splendours). Hated by the rich, whom he intimidated by secret police and taxed ruinously, he was supported by a number of intellectuals—Plato visited him—and by the proletariat on whom he showered benefits : he also liberated thousands of slaves.

When peace with the Carthaginians was concluded after thirteen years' warfare (392), Dionysius I, who possessed great military ability, had penned them in the western corner of Sicily. He also controlled the remaining populations of the island, not only Greeks but the native Sicels of the interior whom he was the first to subdue. The new "Ruler of Sicily", as he called himself, then invaded the toe of Italy and formed numerous alliances further north (as well as intervening to help Sparta against Athens and Thebes). Soon, after ravaging Etruria and Elba and occupying Corsica and perhaps parts of the Adriatic coast, he was the strongest ruler in Europe—and his state was the first great political creation of the Greeks in the west, and the greatest empire the Greeks had ever built. But then Dionysius I entered a fresh war with Carthage (*c.* 383) in which he fared badly, and before retrieving his position he died. The presence of Carthaginian power in Sicily had defeated his ambition to found a central Mediterranean empire. His ineffective successor Dionysius II and his regent Dion lost much ground, but some prosperity was regained under a moderate democracy set up by the Corinthian general Timoleon (344–37).

Dionysius I was expelled by Plato's friend Dion, who then, as regent, became "tyrant in spite of himself"

Carthage made a treaty in 348 with Rome, to which she later lost the Punic Wars (264–146 B.C.)

Dion and Plato —who visited Syracuse twice more— dismally failed in their effort to make Dionysius II the Platonic philosopher king

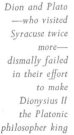

PHILIP OF MACEDON

Philip studied Epaminondas' military methods while a hostage at Thebes (367–4). He devoted special attention to morale

Greece was exhausted and at the mercy of any strong power. Since the early days of Greek history the northern part of the country had been divided among semi-primitive tribal monarchies, including that of the fierce, pastoral, warlike Macedonians. Now Philip II of Macedon (359–36), the greatest general of his day, made his army the most formidable the world had ever seen, and created a powerful, centralised Macedonia. By employing the rich gold mines of Mount Pangaeus he disposed of extensive funds, of which he made abundant use to bribe the Greek cities while threatening, by his new navy, Athenian trade with the Black Sea. The ineffective Sacred War (356–46) between Thebes and its neighbour Phocis (which had seized Delphi and melted down its metal treasures) gave Philip his opportunity to intervene, and he advanced as far as Thermopylae (352). Athens, its diminished resources increased (perhaps threefold) by the able conservative financier Eubulus, opposed Philip there and on the Dardanelles; but it was Eubulus' political opponent, the outstanding orator Demosthenes, who saw the full danger and spent more than a decade in attempting—notably in his great Philippic and Olynthiac speeches—to rouse his fellow-citizens to deal with it.

Philip's army was trained in siege-craft and possessed a flexible, long-piked phalanx, and a cavalry of formidable offensive powers

The speeches of Demosthenes (which are on many subjects) display brilliant clarity and manifest sincerity

Philip was stabbed by an officer at a wedding-party

When Philip raised Euboea in revolt, destroyed Olynthus and dismantled the towns of Phocis, the Athenians made peace (346). But Demosthenes persuaded them to send a fleet to the Dardanelles (342) and rallied Thebes (but few Peloponnesians) against him at the battle of Chaeronea (338). Though the armies were of the same size (about 32,000 men), Philip's generalship easily prevailed, and the whole of Greece was his. He imposed upon it a federal system which obliged the Greeks to settle their quarrels in future by arbitration, and to send delegates to a Hellenic Parliament at Corinth—this League of Corinth to be "in alliance with" Philip. He was appointed commander-in-chief of a national army to invade Persia; and then he was murdered in 336 and was succeeded by Alexander.

The League of Corinth did not represent an important advance towards a national state

⟨ 359–336 B.C. ⟩

EDUCATION AND CYNICISM

Isocrates' school has been called the first European University : it sought to provide a comprehensive education which would improve the character and fit pupils for life (cf. the classics in nineteenth-century education)

There were Athenians who regarded Chaeronea as good news. Among them was one of the most influential educationalists who has ever lived, Isocrates. In 390 he had opened a school at Athens for the training of orators and politicians. This not only created a new, elaborate basis for prose style, it became a centre of Panhellenism : he saw no way to establish peace unless the Greeks could regard themselves as a nation, and unless Sparta and Athens, each compromising on its aims, should lead them against Persia. He successively appealed to Dionysius of Syracuse (368), Archidamus of Sparta (356) and Philip of Macedon (346) to take the initiative in a great eastern expedition. A few days before his death at the age of ninety-eight he wrote to Philip congratulating him on his victory at Chaeronea.

Isocrates maintained that the only proper Greeks were those educated at Athens

Diogenes crowned himself with a victor's pine-wreath, claiming victory over poverty, disgrace, anger, grief, desire, fear, and, above all, pleasure

There were others who dissociated themselves more completely from the happenings of this troubled period, which saw the end of so much of the ancient pattern of life. Diogenes (c. 400–325), the son of a rich banker of Sinope (in northern Asia Minor), came to Athens as an exile in about the middle of the fourth century. Like Plato, he believed that virtue was all-important, but he went further and saw no difference, except in virtue, between Greek and barbarian, rich and poor, master and slave, wise and foolish. He claimed that a man ought to devote himself wholeheartedly to "training for virtue", i.e. he ought to assert his complete independence of society and renounce his possessions, thus living happily even in war and disorder—only satisfying his natural needs and satisfying them in the cheapest and simplest way.

Diogenes carried his asceticism (askesis) to the extent of eating his food raw and sleeping in a tub—where Alexander paid him his famous visit

Diogenes himself lived in the most beggarly way possible, and was nicknamed the "dog" (*kyon*, hence *cynic*) because these beliefs led to "shameless-ness" ; what is natural cannot be indecent or degrading, and should therefore be done in public. According to one tradition, Diogenes called himself a "cosmopolitan"—as an exile he was only a citizen of the *cosmos* (universe), like so many other displaced persons of the century. Though Diogenes formed no school, his disciples comforted many in perilous, poverty-stricken times, and the Cynic conception of the philosopher as the man who is imperturbable and impervious to circumstances was to dominate great masses of the populations of the Graeco-Roman world.

The Stoics helped to hand on many Cynic doctrines

PART FOUR
AFTER 336 B.C.
THE DIFFUSION OF GREEK IDEAS

Alexander conquers half the world—it is Hellenised under his successors—Greek scientific and philosophic systems develop—Christianity spreads in Greek lands under Rome—Greece rules again through Byzantium—Tsarist Russia the heir of its autocracy—the Italian Renaissance revives ancient Greek humanism—Greece offers something different to every generation since.

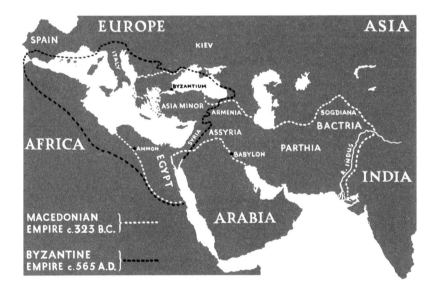

ALEXANDER THE GREAT

Alexander was the first and last western conqueror of Afghanistan

He died at Babylon of a fever after a two-night drinking bout, in his thirty-third year

Philip's son and successor Alexander the Great (336–23) briskly secured Macedonia, Greece and his northern frontiers, and then (334) undertook the task he had inherited from his father—the destruction of the Persian empire. In his astonishing Odyssey he conquered the entire Persian territory in five years (334–29), and extended the frontiers of his kingdom as far as Russian Turkestan and the Punjab, calling a halt only when his Macedonian troops refused to follow him farther. His return journey was marked by terrible losses in the heat of the south Persian deserts.

Principal victories of Alexander (334–31): Granicus on Dardanelles, Issus, Tyre, Gaugamela

At the time of his death he was planning a marine expedition to open the sea route from Babylon to Egypt round the coast of Arabia

Unlike the Persians, Alexander led his army from the front

Alexander reputedly founded seventy Alexandrias; the greatest in Egypt

Alexander's conquests helped to break down the ancient dialects into a new uniform language (koine)

Alexander adopted the remarkable policy of declaring himself successor of Darius III as Great King, using Persian royal ceremonial, and marrying into the Iranian aristocracy. Evidently he intended that his empire should not be a Macedonian autocracy but a partnership between Macedonians and Persians. This did not please his independent Macedonian military men, nor certain Greek city-states when they were requested to treat him as a god—as great benefactors and heroes were customarily venerated. His empire was too large to be tranquil, and his last years saw a mutiny in Babylonia, risings of Greek soldiers settled in Afghanistan, and threats of warfare back in Greece.

Hot-headed and sometimes brutal, Alexander killed his close Macedonian associates Parmenio and Critias

Alexander perhaps derived his inspiration from a mystic belief in his own divine mission and in his spiritual kinship to Dionysus, Heracles and Jupiter Ammon. A general of unprecedented quality, with a deep, almost instinctive strategic and tactical mastery, he made the fullest use of the magnificent army he had inherited. He possessed exceptional talents as a cavalry leader, and flawless personal courage. The calibre of his statesmanship is disputed, but he displayed outstanding political and economic insight by the founding of his many Alexandrias, some of them far to the east.

He made a special trip to Jupiter's desert oracle while in Egypt

Lysippus of Sicyon created from Alexander's features a new sculptural ideal

This colonisation helped to bring about the pre-eminent result of his career—the extension of a homogeneous Greek civilisation over the east. This extension, and the flood of Persian gold it released, meant a change in the centre of gravity. Greece itself and its city-states were now of secondary importance.

As the city-states waned, social clubs increased

⟨ 336–323 B.C. ⟩

ARISTOTLE

Alexander sent
to Athens
records of the
Asian flora and
fauna, made by
his staff
of scientists, for
examination by
the Peripatetics

The giant temporal stature of Alexander is equalled by the spiritual stature of his mentor in youth, Aristotle (384–22). An Ionian from Stagira, he was a pupil of Plato at Athens for the last twenty years of Plato's life. Later he became tutor to Alexander, and while the latter was in Asia, Aristotle taught at Athens, where he founded the "Peripatetic" school. After Alexander's death he was ejected as a pro-Macedonian and died soon afterwards at Chalcis in Euboea.

Peripatos—a
covered walking
place in a
gymnasium,
where Aristotle
gave serious
lectures in the
morning and
popular talks in
the afternoon

Aristotle's
surviving treatises
were not
prepared for
publication but
are rather
lecture
memoranda

Aristotle gradually developed from Platonic otherworldliness to an increasingly scientific interest in the phenomena of this world, and to the conviction that speculation must be based on their systematic investigation. In his works on Logic he was the first to develop the science of reasoning (scientific and formal) based on the "syllogism". In his *Metaphysics* he examined the basis of the universe, and in many works on Natural Philosophy the constituent elements of nature, movement of the stars, weather phenomena and animal life. His two works on *Ethics* mainly investigate the end to which human conduct should be directed. The ideal, he concludes, is the contemplation of philosophic truth, but the ordinary man must find his happiness in moral goodness and practical wisdom : he distinguishes between moral and intellectual qualities, and identifies the moral ideal as a Mean between two extremes of conduct. His *Politics* is based on the assumption that city-states give men the best lives, though—owing to Philip and Alexander—the day of the city-state was almost done. Aristotle's *Rhetoric*, by systematising that greatly influential art or science, exercised a profound influence on later Graeco-Roman taste and education. But it was on philosophers and scientists that he exerted the greatest influence. His outstanding qualities were his powerful commonsense and an orderliness which has handed down to us the basis, and much of the terminology, of our scientific classifications.

Aristotle's Mean
was a
philosophical
restatement of
that moderation
("nothing too
much") which
had for
centuries
pervaded the
thought of the
often all too
immoderate
Greeks. It led
to the idealism
of moderation
of Cicero and
Horace

Aristotle believed
slavery to be
natural

Aristotle's
Poetics
dominated
European literary
criticism for
two millennia

Aristotle's
philosophy
dominated the
curricula of
mediaeval
universities,
which it reached
mainly through
Latin versions of
Arabic versions

E.g. A Mean
between
asceticism and
debauchery

⟨ 336–322 B.C. ⟩

ENLIGHTENED MONARCHY

Alexander's son by Roxana was murdered in 310–09

Alexander's death was followed by over forty years of warfare between his generals. By 280 B.C. three huge cosmopolitan kingdoms had taken shape. The Antigonids ruled in the Balkans, the Seleucids from the Aegean to the Hindu Kush, and the Ptolemies in Egypt and southern Syria.

This is the "Hellenistic" age

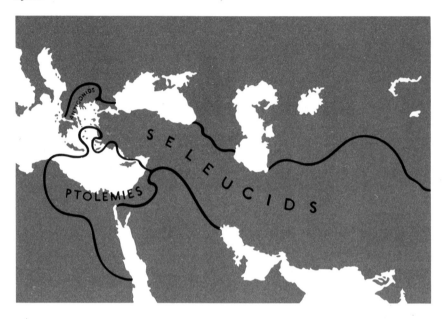

Antigonus was the grandson of a general of Alexander. He invited eminent Stoics to his court

This sort of kingship appealed to the Macedonians as reminiscent of the good old days of Philip, before oriental ways had intruded

In Macedonia, after a temporary eclipse by King Pyrrhus of Epirus (297–72) and the overrunning of most of the Balkans by the Celtic Galatians (279), the monarchy was revived by Antigonus Gonatas (276–41), one of the noblest of the Hellenistic kings and the monarch who (with Asoka and Marcus Aurelius) most nearly put philosophy into practice. Blunt, sarcastic, he refused to allow himself to be worshipped —he practised, and perhaps invented, the doctrine that kingship meant service : he called it "a glorious slavery", i.e. a job of hard work which seems glorious to the world. This semi-philosophical basis of the Macedonian monarch gave many a hint to later Roman emperors. The Macedonian people, unlike a city-state Assembly, were not sovereign ; a self-willed Macedonian monarch acted by himself, but Antigonus Gonatas was conscientious in his respect for the people's interests. The Antigonids protected Hellenism against the barbarians of the north. Many Greek states, though still self-governing, depended on Macedonia. Others, for mutual defence, extended federal institutions beyond merely kindred peoples : the Achaean League (280–146) in most of the Peloponnese, and the Aetolian League from the Adriatic to the Aegean.

The Aetolian League provided for overseas members

THE SELEUCID EMPIRE

Alexander's general Seleucus (*d.* 280) established himself in territories extending from the Aegean to the Indus. Like Alexander, he envisaged a Graeco-Iranian character for his realms; but unlike Alexander he and his successors depended principally on Greek immigrants. The Seleucids were absolute monarchs, and they were constantly at war. Grappling with overwork and separatist movements, they endeavoured with some success to preserve their huge, heterogeneous realm from anarchy and raise its standard of living. The many Greek cities of their empire, new and old, possessed a wide measure of autonomy and were endowed by the king with much land—thereby improving the condition of the serfs, many of whom rose to the status of hereditary settlers. Steps were taken towards a great extension of Hellenism in Asia Minor.

At the peripheries of the Seleucid empire, important areas broke away and formed independent kingdoms. In the west, Eumenes of Pergamum founded the businesslike, bureaucratic Attalid kingdom (262) which lasted for 130 years—despite discontent among its Greek subjects—and produced some of the greatest artistic masterpieces of the Hellenistic age.

Of the first fourteen Seleucid kings, only two died peacefully at home

Seleucus and his son Antiochus were great town builders. Seleucus' greatest foundation was his new, cosmopolitan capital, Antioch

Eumenes threw off Seleucid allegiance with Egyptian help

Best known Pergamene sculpture is the "Dying Gaul"

The Pergamene school of sculpture displays the quintessence of contemporary technical virtuosity, with its restless feeling after new styles, theatrical attitudes and realism of detail. At the other extremity of the empire, Bactria and Sogdiana became an independent quasi-national country under Euthydemus of Magnesia (*c.* 230), who invented a new state form by allotting lands to his relatives as sub-kings. Euthydemus never encroached on Seleucid territory, but his son Demetrius conquered the Seleucid provinces of the Persian desert and a huge area of north India. The art of this Indo-Greek court was Greek, but the kingdom was separated from other Greek lands by the rising Iranian empire of the Parthians who seized its Bactrian half, while the Indian areas were overrun by central Asian invaders (*c.* 80–30 B.C.).

The public buildings of Pergamum, rising in terraces to the acropolis, were a masterpiece of town planning

Demetrius' successor Menander ruled India from Mathura to Kathiawar, and became a Buddhist legend

STATE CONTROL IN EGYPT

The Ptolemaic dynasty ruled in Egypt from 323 to 30 B.C. They are better known to us than any other Hellenistic dynasty because of the great modern discoveries of papyri in their country

Alexander's general Ptolemy, son of Lagus, obtained possession of Egypt. His descendants (Lagids) emerge as practical, hard-headed, tenacious men who knew supremely well how to exploit, without disaster, their country and its peoples. Yet, like the Seleucids, they sought to endow their autocracy with a philosophic basis : the duty of the king is to duplicate the Order of the universe. In the eyes of the non-Greek inhabitants of Egypt, however, their rule was merely a change of masters. The Ptolemies proved able to control, tactfully enough, the great vested interests of priesthood and temple. They also organised great voyages of exploration to the east and south.

Ptolemy II (283–46) established an economic system which is the most thorough-going instance of state control in the ancient world. The state—i.e. the autocratic monarch—owned all the land and nearly all the means of production, and controlled all business (by monopolies or on a percentage basis). The result was an enormous bureaucracy, whose decreasing standards of honesty caused grave unrest in the second century B.C. There were many riots and departures to the maquis in the marshes ; the government was oppressive and less ethical than those of the other great states. Yet Egypt remained productive, and Alexandria—inheriting the trade of Tyre—became the centre of a new commerce between Europe and the east, and grew enormously in wealth and importance.

The ancient port of Tyre was destroyed by Alexander and its population scattered

Without the poets of the Alexandrian school, the great Roman poets Catullus, Virgil and Horace could never have achieved their mature excellences of language and rhythm

No single one of the great states possessed a monopoly of Hellenistic culture, but, under Ptolemaic care, Alexandria soon rivalled Athens as the cultural centre of the western world. Ptolemy I established the epoch-making Library (of 100,000 to 700,000 volumes) where the outstanding scholars of the day held posts and studied. In this atmosphere rose the Alexandrian school of Greek poetry (c. 300–260) with a highly finished style, much experiment in literary forms, metres and themes, and a new concentration on the individual. This movement produced considerable poets in Callimachus, Apollonius and Theocritus : the two last named evolved the new forms of the "romantic epic" and the "pastoral".

Ptolemy II greatly extended the library

The city-state no longer provided a satisfactory background, and the large states were too remote to provide a social setting for poetry

SCIENCE IN ALEXANDRIA

*Ptolemy himself
wrote the best
history of
Alexander*

Ptolemy I also founded the Museum—housing one hundred state-paid research scholars from all parts of the Mediterranean. Their work was partly intended to combat current anti-monarchist and socialist theories. But Ptolemy himself was a genuine lover of learning. The third century saw great scientific advances ; the Greeks remained, on the whole, theoreticians (and indeed philosophers) rather than scientists, and so excelled particularly in mathematics. Archimedes, the greatest engineer and mathematician of antiquity, invented hydrostatics ; and Euclid, determined to understand as a rational system the laws of measuring the earth, produced his "Elements" and superseded all predecessors in Geometry.

*Characteristic of
these Greeks,
Archimedes
expressed his
contempt for
the practical
applications of
science*

*"Bridge of asses" :
an obstacle
for the
dull-witted
in Euclid
whose works
continued to
provide basic
instruction in
Geometry for
more than two
thousand years*

In other sciences, Herophilus discovered the nerves, understood that they centred on the brain, and—anticipating Harvey—virtually discovered the circulation of the blood. Erasistratus clearly distinguished the motor and sensory nerves. Aristarchus anticipated Copernicus by his brilliant unsupported guess that the earth went round the sun. Hipparchus—the greatest Greek astronomer—disbelieved him, but made systematic use of trigonometry and probably discovered the Precession of the Equinoxes. After Pytheas had circumnavigated Britain—and discovered that the moon, not the sun, caused the tides—Eratosthenes created scientific geography (and added a suggestion of land across the Atlantic).

*Pytheas
discovered
Albion (Britain),
Ierne (Ireland),
and Thule
(? Ireland or
Norway)*

*Hipparchus
catalogued and
located 850
stars, and
accurately
calculated the
mean lunar
month*

*This lighthouse
on the isle of
Pharos was the
prototype of
all lighthouses.
It was long
considered one
of the Seven
Wonders of the
World*

Agricultural experts, with many text-books to their credit, enabled Ptolemaic Egypt to introduce its controlled economy. Architects achieved such innovations as Alexandria's great underground cisterns and 400-foot lighthouse. Ctesiphus invented a water-clock and a catapult worked by compressed air. Hero, later, wrote of many inventions operating by steam, water and compressed air. However, chemistry (except for alchemy), physics, zoology and botany made little progress. In general, by the second century B.C. science had ceased to be a real force and had come to be thought a dilettante study for the moneyed minority. It was not systematically applied to production ; and in a hard world it seemed less interesting than the individual's ethics.

*A later Greek,
Galen of
Pergamum
(A.D. 129–
? 199),
dominated
subsequent
European
medicine*

*Alexandrians
created ecology
and climatology,
and wrote on
agriculture,
fruit trees,
gardens, bee-
keeping, horse
breeding, drill
and tactics,
fishing, gems,
gastronomy and
cosmetics*

SCEPTICS AND EPICUREANS

Pyrrho, a painter, had accompanied Alexander to the east

The sceptical parodist Timon, and members of Plato's academy, ridiculed dogmatic philosophies —with great effect on Graeco-Roman thought

Rejection of most conventions had been preached by Diogenes the Cynic. A generation later, when the world had been transformed by Alexander, Pyrrho of Elis (c. 360–270), forerunner of the Sceptics, was even more radical. Like Diogenes, they aimed at peace of mind, but they felt it must be achieved by understanding the universe and our relation to it : yet certainty about such matters being impossible, our "understanding" must take the form of refraining from vain speculation, and suspending our judgment. This suspense between "yes" and "no" will create in our souls a comparable equilibrium which will liberate us from our cares by producing absolute indifference as far as outward things are concerned.

Scepticism did good by exploding untenable beliefs and attacking the irrational element in public life

Athens was "freed" in 228 after losing her independence to Macedonia (262)

Athens, though now of secondary importance in the political field, was still the home of great philosophical schools. To Plato's Academy and Aristotle's Peripatetics were soon added the schools of the Epicureans and the Stoics. Epicurus of Athens (c. 342–270) regarded sense-perception as the one and only basis of knowledge. The truth, to him, lay in the atomic theory of Democritus, but he rejected the wholly mechanical view by giving atoms the power of swerving a little in order to meet and clash, i.e. he gave them (and human beings who are composed of atoms) free will. Yet Epicurus was a determined materialist and wished by his atomic system to liberate mankind from the fear of death and divinity. This was his way of working towards the peace of mind which, in a new age in which man is alone, defenceless and afraid in the world, was the ideal of Hellenistic philosophies. Led by his trust in sensations, Epicurus argued that the highest good and supreme human aim is *happiness*—by which he meant pleasure, but primarily pleasure of a negative kind : renunciation, independence, imperturbability, freedom from trouble and pain.

Epicurus also symbolised the impotence of the city-state, not only by denying its religion but by advising withdrawal from public life : "Avoid love, marriage, having children, avarice, public life, careerism"

With his disbelief in culture, he did not exercise a very far-reaching effect on Graeco-Roman intelligentsia, though—on a superficial level—what passed for Epicureanism became current in extrovert circles. But he foreshadowed the Social Contract by envisaging law as a practical agreement against violence.

Curiously, the views of simple friendly Epicurus were reproduced in the vivid Roman poetry of the isolated, fanatical, majestic Lucretius (first century B.C.)

⟨ 320–270 B.C. ⟩

STOICISM

A deliberately opposed attempt at imperturbability was made by the Stoics, teaching in the Painted Porch (*stoa*) at Athens *c.* 300–207, and led successively by Zeno of Citium, Cleanthes and Chrysippus. The Stoics like other Hellenistic philosophers were products of the new individualistic world created by the eclipse of the city-states. Practical conduct was more directly their concern than abstract truth, and they held that man's inmost self is defensible against all threats—he is the captain of his own soul. That is the Stoic version of the Hellenistic spirit which set up imperturbability—single-minded staunchness—as a high ideal. Their teaching *live consistently with nature* was meant ethically. In opposition to the Epicureans they held that the universe was animated by a divine spark, the *Logos*, Mind, or Zeus, of which all human beings have a share and so can attain to its goodness. Taking little interest in science or abstract thought, they maintained that the prime duty of the soul was to realise its perfectibility. Where the basic feeling by earlier Greek ethics had been potentiality—*you can*, the Stoics were the first to introduce the moral imperative—*you must*. Conscience and duty were the keynotes of Stoic ethics. Yet the early Stoics were fatalists, envisaging a divine universal Law of Nature, binding on all men—but all men were therefore brothers and the Stoics proclaimed the universal brotherhood of Man, with justice belonging to all men as the citizens of the world-state, the *cosmopolis*.

In pursuance of this untroubled calm, the Stoic could not admit sympathy with a sufferer

This is a new sort of dogma, ethical in character

The Stoics taught that the effort must incessantly be made to perfect human nature, and nothing else is of any real importance

Alexander had experimented with the practical development of Macedonian-Persian brotherhood

Such doctrines evidently had anti-nationalistic, anti-class implications. It seems probable that these played a large part in the social unrest and slave-risings that almost cracked the structure of the Mediterranean world in the third and second centuries B.C. Yet it is very doubtful if the founders of Stoicism had revolutionary intentions : it was virtue and divinity, not wealth, of which they proclaimed that men had an equal share ; men are equal because they can be equal in their souls.

The Stoic Law of Nature greatly influenced Roman law

The humane, individualistic ideas of Hellenistic philosophers at Athens found early expression in the New Comedy of Menander (*c.* 341–290)— a comedy of manners, witty, polished, sympathetic, in a minor key, interested in persons, not city-states : it became the ancestor of the whole of European comic drama.

"Nothing could prevent some seats in the theatre being better than others" (Chrysippus)

⟨ **300–100 B.C.** ⟩

RELIGIOUS ESCAPISM

In Hellenistic religion, which dominated the Mediterranean world at the time of Christ, the characteristic divinity was Fortune: she represented the order of events which everyone could see but few could understand. The terrible ravages of Chance caused millions to seek escape from it in Fate and oriental astrology. From the east, largely from Syria and Asia Minor, came the emotional mystery religions with their initiations which also offered escape from Fate by promising salvation in the next world.

Millions sought escape from both Chance and Fate in magic. In the second century magic from Assyria, Asia, Persia, Babylon and Judaea met in Egypt, and soon flooded into the west

Now, to the old Greek cults of Demeter and Dionysus were added the rapidly spreading, emotional, oriental cults, notably that of the Anatolian earth-mother Cybele with her drama of the death and rebirth of her consort Attis, god of things that grow. Most powerful and widespread of all was the dramatic worship of the Egyptian moon-goddess Isis, with her fertility-god consort Osiris, god of the underworld, and the jackal-headed Anubis, conductor of souls to immortal life: for immortality was what this Egyptian cult promised above all—and the presiding goddess Isis made a powerful appeal to women (something new to Hellenism). Especially attractive to men (particularly to army officers) was the cult of the Indo-Iranian sun-god Mithras, whose sternly virile and austere rejection of all weakness provided the non-philosophical route to the Hellenistic goal: imperviousness to circumstances.

The Hellenistic peoples—except in Macedonia—also worshipped their rulers, because they seemed superior to other men. The Ptolemies and Seleucids received not only private adulation but official worship from the chief priests of their capitals. Yet ruler-worship was very different from the emotional mystery faiths, being mainly political and containing little emotion, but gratitude or reverence for a personage who was remote but so powerful that he truly seemed *Benefactor* (Euergetes), *God made Manifest* (Epiphanes), and *Saviour* (Soter). In 300 B.C. Euhemerus of Messene had explained that the gods had originally been men—great kings whom men had worshipped out of gratitude. The Stoics, too, taught that man, by virtue of his reason, had divinity in him and the innate capacity to become a god. It was the Jews, however, and later the Christians who spread the conception of the "otherness" of God.

THE ROMAN CONQUESTS

*Infanticide
became very
common in the
third and second
centuries B.C.*

*Sicily became a
Roman province
after the first
of Rome's three
victories over
Carthage
(241 B.C.)*

In the fourth century the Succession States of Alexander had a surplus of population ; in the third century this vanished. It had become harder to rear children since the value of money deteriorated, and the resources of the Mediterranean world were frittered away by constant warfare. The gap between rich and poor continued to grow wider ; there was an ever-increasing destitute proletariat, slave markets swelled, and from 279 onwards unrest and outbreaks occurred among slaves and proletariat.

The Hellenistic monarchies were no match for Rome—their phalanx and hoplites could not compete with the legions—and in due course they were absorbed by her. The Macedonian kings were defeated at Cynoscephalae (196) and Pydna (168), and their country was annexed in 146 B.C. The Seleucid expansionist Antiochus III was checked at Thermopylae and Magnesia (190), and the Seleucid empire, reduced to a small area of Syria, came to an end in 63 B.C. The last king of Pergamum, Attalus III, bequeathed his kingdom to Rome in 133, but the Romans only took possession of it after a savage local outburst of the class warfare characteristic of the period. Egypt, after its share of disturbances (and a period of virtual subjection to Rome), experienced a brief, remarkable recovery under Cleopatra VII, who attracted Caesar and captivated Antony before her kingdom too was annexed by Rome in 30 B.C. Then there were no important Hellenistic states left.

*Alexander's
release of the
Persian treasure
had helped to
inaugurate a long
period in which
prices rose,
sometimes very
steeply*

*The island of
Delos had a huge
slave market,
capable of
handling 10,000
a day (Asians,
Syrians, Jews,
Egyptians,
Greeks)*

*The Aetolian
League became
subject allies of
Rome in 189
B.C. The
Achaean League
ceased to exist as
a separate unit
in 146*

*"The pulse of
the Roman empire
was driven by
a Greek heart"
(Arnold Toynbee)*

Yet "captured Greece took her conqueror captive" : the culture of eastern cities remained Greek, and Rome's administration of these territories absorbed many features already existing—indeed the Roman empire has been described as a federation of city-states : and Christianity, spreading among its peoples, was a potent Hellenising force.

*Christianity
owed much to
Stoic concern for
humanity, as
well as to Jewish
religion*

⟨ 300 B.C.–A.D. 330 ⟩

BYZANTIUM AND THE RENAISSANCE

Byzantium, renamed Constantinopolis by the Roman emperor Constantine the Great (306–337), fell to the Turks in 1453

Byzantine art profoundly affected the west. There was continuity, rather than a break, between Middle Ages and Renaissance

Renaissance Italy modelled its city-states on Greece

A great intermediary between classical studies and Christianity had been St Augustine (A.D. 354–430)

The Byzantine Empire, Rome's Christian and partly orientalised successor, was Greek in language and many aspects of its culture. By its transmission of this inheritance, Greek thought, art, letters, religion and law fundamentally influenced Russia, where the baptism of Vladimir (988) led the way to the Byzantinised Orthodox Church. Similarly the autocracies of Alexander's successors, with Byzantium as intermediary, left many traces on the Tsarist régime, and through it on Soviet Russia.

From the ninth century there were strong links with Kiev

Greek philosophy and science had come to the west through the Muslims in Spain and elsewhere

The Humanists learnt of the Stoics from Cicero

Greeks came west as diplomats, or refugees from the Turks

In the west, Greek traditions were revived and adapted to the intellectual and social developments of the Renaissance. The Stoic Brotherhood of Man, which had played its part in early Christianity, inspired the Humanists. It was also widely felt that man's achievements were best, indeed only, available through the ancient literatures. So Greek, as well as Latin, was ardently sought. Petrarch (1304–74) learnt a little Greek from a monk; Boccaccio brought to their native Florence its first teacher of Greek and learnt it himself; and in the next century Guarino and Poggio were pupils of Manuel Chrysoloras from Constantinople.

Erasmus (1466–1536) from the Low Countries was among those who spread the knowledge of Greek at Oxford and Cambridge, and his many works included an edition of the Greek Testament.

The Renaissance acquired, filtered through Rome, the principal elements in Greek architecture and sculpture.. Western progress in science and mathematics during the sixteenth and seventeenth centuries could never have been made without the Greeks.

The Parthenon   *Birmingham Town Hall*

WE AND THE GREEKS

The nineteenth century witnessed a keen revival of interest in all things Greek. But its students, for all their immense contributions to classical research, developed certain assumptions which might hinder our understanding today:

1   That we should have liked to live in a Greek city-state, and that fifth-century Athens— aggression, slavery and all—was perfect.

2   That, its leaders being almost identical with well-bred English gentlemen, the study of Hellenism is primarily an aristocratic study.

3   That Greek wars were pleasant little affairs.

4   That there was no other memorable ancient civilisation (except that of the Jews) east of the Greeks.

The romantics wrongly believed the Romans to be mere imitators

5   That the ancient literatures are more important for their language than for their content.

Good readable translations now exist

6   But that their translations may be written in boringly pedantic English, full of ancient technical terms.

7   That the Greeks were pallid, anaemic people with pre-Raphaelite goitres, or equivocal, faun-like creatures dancing through the glades.

"Even a quick walk was opposed to their decorum" (Winckelmann, 1717–68)

Greek standards were splendidly high, though they often fell below them (e.g. by lying and behaving irrationally)

Ancient Greece and its literature not only contributed vitally to past stages of our civilisation, but are also directly relevant to our problems today.   For instance:

1   No people has ever displayed so compulsive an urge toward finding out, by vigorous rational thinking, the truth.

2   Their enormously varied literature and art often achieve outstanding beauty.

3   Their humanity contributed much to Christianity, of which Greece provided the background.

4   Conversely, ancient Greece supplied elements from which important features of Soviet Russia are derived.

5   The classical civilisation, which Greece originated, is the only civilisation which is spread out before us, adequately recorded, from beginning to end.

"Nothing too much" is relevant to the atomic age

6   Greek ideals of freedom, self-control and public service are of permanent significance.

Can Greece guide us to avoid similar mistakes, for instance futile wars?

⟨ A.D. 1750–1958 ⟩

THE END

"Atom" and "Physics" are Greek words,
"Hydrogen" Greek derived